ARMIES
OF THE WORLD
1854·1914

ARMIES
OF THE WORLD
1854-1914
DAVID WOODWARD

G. P. Putnam's Sons New York

Acknowledgments

The author and publishers are grateful to the following for permission to quote from, or to adapt material from, their copyright material: Cassell & Collier Macmillan Ltd, for *The Civil War Dictionary* by Colonel Mark Mayo Boatner III; Almark Publishing Co., for *Austro-Hungarian Infantry, 1914-18* by J. S. Lucas; Harvard University Press for *Yamagata Aritomo in the Rise of Modern Japan* by R. F. Hackett; University of Oklahoma for *The Lost Cause* by Andrew F. Rolle; Rupert Furneaux for *The Siege of Plevna*, published in Great Britain by Blond and Briggs (and in the United States by Thomas Y. Crowell under the title *The Breakfast War)*; Charles Scribner's Sons for *Robert E. Lee* by D. S. Freeman; Charles E. Wingo III, First and Merchant's National Bank, Richmond, Virginia for *Lee's Lieutenants*; David Higham Associates for *A Short History of the British Army* by Major E. W. Sheppard (published by Constable & Co.); the Government of India, Ministry of Education and Social Welfare for *1857* by Dr S. N. Sen; and Anthony Sheil Associates Ltd, for *A Matter of Honour* and *The Men Who Ruled India*, both by Philip Mason (published by Jonathan Cape). They would also like to thank Peter Lum and Musketoon of Woodstock.

Front end-papers: Union infantry outside Fredricksburg in 1865, during the American Civil War.
Page 5: Colour Sergeant William McGregor of the Scots Fusilier Guards.
Pages 6 and 7: Foreign attachés at the 1911 Kaiser manoeuvres. Standing from left to right: German, Belgian, Bolivian, Turkish, Russian. Sitting from left to right: Spanish, French, German, Greek, Rumanian, Japanese and Chilean.
Pages 8 and 9: The 9th Battery of the Cheshire Brigade at Aberysthwyth in 1910, soon after the introduction of khaki uniforms.
Rear end-papers: Prussian troops in Paris during the Franco-Prussian War, March 1871.

Photographic Acknowledgements

Photographs have been supplied, or are reproduced, by kind permission of the following people and organizations: Army Historical Museum, Vienna, 59; K. Brownlow, 149/1; G. A. Embleton, 132, 133, 134-5, 136, 139, 141, 142/2; Historical Research Unit, 6-7, 8-9, 25/1, 25/2, 28, 29/1, 30/1, 30/2, 31/1, 31/2, 32-3, 34-5, 36, 37/1, 37/2, 46, 48, 49/2, 57/1, 57/2, 60/1, 60-1, 78, 84-5, 84/2, 85/2, 86-7, 89, 90, 95/1, 95/2, 96, 114-5, 151/1, 172/1, 172/2, 174, 175; Imperial War Museum, 5, 116, 117; P. Katcher, 138, 142/1, 145/1, 148/1, 148/2, 151/2; Library of Congress, 142/3, 151/3; Mollo Collection, 38/2, 62/2, 64-5, 64/2, 65/2, 66, 67/1, 67/2, 67/3, 68/1, 74-5, 76/1, 76/2, 77/1, 77/2, 80, 100, 102/1, 102/2, 104, 112-3, 145/2, 158/1, 158/2; National Army Museum, 38/1, 39, 72, 97, 106-7, 108/1, 108/2, 110/1, 110/2, 110-1, 118, 120-1/1, 120-1/2, 123, 124-5, 126-7, 150, 157, 159, 161, 167, 168/1, 168/2, 169/1, 169/2, 186; Novosti, 62/1, 62-3, 68/2, 69, 71/1, 71/2, 76/3, 77/3; Popperfoto, 20-1/1, 20-1/2, 22, 25/3, 26-7, 41, 50, 52-3, 54-5, 61/1, 171; Radio Times Hulton Picture Library, rear end-papers; Roger-Viollet, 29/2, 40, 42, 43, 44, 45, 47, 49/1; U.S. Signal Corps, front end-papers, 128, 131/1, 131/2, 131/3, 131/4, 144/1, 144-5, 147, 148-9.

Copyright © 1978 David Woodward

Designed by Paul Watkins
Picture Research by the Historical Research Unit
Library of Congress Catalog Card Number: 78-60254
SBN: 399-12252-4

Printed in Great Britain

CONTENTS

INTRODUCTION

On 20 September 1854, the British, French and Turkish armies went into action against the Russians on the River Alma in the first battle of the Crimean campaign. They advanced in a huge, closely packed mass, four miles wide and four miles deep, 60,000 strong, in the most extravagant finery of military full dress, hardly distinguishable from that of the Napoleonic Wars which had ended forty years previously. As they advanced now up the hill, towards the waiting Russians, they made the air sweet with the scent of the grass they trampled under foot.

It was the end of an age.

Within a few years a spectacle as that of the allies on the Alma would be impossible, for with the lengthening range of small arms and artillery such a concentration of infantry or cavalry would not be able to live within sight of a well-armed foe. A new style of warfare had to develop and did develop fully during the American Civil War, when the practice of war made its first great leap forward since Napoleon I.

The battle of the Alma was the warfare of Wellington, perhaps even of Marlborough. The fighting of the American Civil War anticipated the First World War, providing situations quite outside the experience of Wellington and Marlborough, but within those of Ludendorff and Foch.

The Civil War and the Crimean War stand both at the end of an age and the beginning of an age. The industrial revolution was taking over Europe and Europe was building up to a state of endemic crisis. The revolutions of 1848 had broken up the peace established by the Congress of Vienna, and old and new ambitions for national self-determination and aggrandizement had been let loose. In the cause of what was considered national security, purse-strings were untied for the acquisition of weapons and the provision of a complex infrastructure which henceforward was essential for the waging of a modern war. This took place at the time when industry was just becoming able to develop and supply what was required. In the Crimea the first of the revolutionary novelties then appearing were steamships — some of them armoured — railways, and the telegraph.

The state of the European telegraph system at this time is shown by the way in which news of the allied victory on the Alma reached London. First the despatch was sent to Constantinople by steamer, where the British Embassy entrusted it to a messenger who rode with it for seven days over the Balkan mountains to the nearest telegraph office, Belgrade, and the news finally arrived in London on the evening of Saturday 30 September, ten days after the battle. The next step was its distribution. The Duke of Newcastle, Secretary for War, sent for Mr Harrison, the publisher of the *London Gazette,* and put the problem to him. The two men then decided to print a special *Gazette,* copies of which were sent round to the London theatres to be read to the audiences from the stage. There was great enthusiasm and not until many days later was it learned that this first report had considerably exaggerated the allied success. With the revised despatch came the casualty lists, containing the names of 3000 British and 1000 French killed or wounded.

After this a cable was laid linking the Crimea with Varna, and Varna with the European telegraph network as a whole. The consequence was not always of benefit to the allied commanders in the field, and the French suffered particularly in this respect. Napoleon III, who was anxious to go out to the Crimea himself and refurbish the laurels won by his uncle, discovered the delights of long-range strategy and made the life of his commander, General Canrobert, such a misery that he resigned, agreeing to serve under the new Commander-in-Chief, General Pelissier. This officer was of sterner stuff, carrying off matters with a high hand, even refusing to be discouraged by the fact that his legs were so short that he could not stay on a horse with comfort and, instead, went trotting about the camp and the battlefield by horse and trap.

The extension of the telegraph network also made the work of the war correspondent — another innovation for the first time fully exploited in this war — much easier. William Russell of *The Times* went to the Crimea without any facilities or hindrances from the army, and proceeded to send a series of uncensored despatches which made history by the criticisms they contained of the muddle and stupidity with which the campaign was being conducted. This aroused much resentment and Russell was accused of sending information which would be of value to the enemy. Here he defended himself on the ground that he left it to Delane, his editor, to decide what should be published. The security problem was made more important by the fact that it was alleged that at this time the London papers reached the Russians in Sevastopol before they reached Lord Raglan, the British Commander-in-Chief, outside the town.

Ill-feeling between the press and senior officers became henceforward an institution as far as the British army was concerned. It was not until the latter half of the Second World War that Montgomery showed that the press could be used as a source of strength for an army instead of being a necessary evil.

In the Crimea it was Russell who told people in Britain of the atrocious state of affairs caused by the callous inefficiency of the military authorities, and it was he who was the main driving force in the campaign for reform, an invaluable ally to Florence Nightingale.

Historians tend to blame Lord Raglan for the poor showing of the British army in the Crimean War. His main fault seems to have been his failure to impress upon the Cabinet at home the defects in organization and supply, which so undermined the fighting ability of the troops. Raglan was sixty-six when the campaign began, and his formative years had been spent under the shadow of the Duke of Wellington during the Napoleonic Wars. Raglan still retained the embarrassing habit of referring to the enemy as the French.

Sixty-six would be a great age for a general in the field nowadays, but this was not so in the middle years of the nineteenth century, which were very much a time for old generals. The Austrian Field-Marshal Radetzky died in command of an army corps at the age of ninety-two, on the eve of his country's war with France in 1859. When the American Civil War began the Commanding General of the United States Army, General Winfield Scott, was seventy-five. Within a few months he had resigned, but not before he had outlined the grand strategy, called the Anaconda Plan, which in the end brought victory to the Union.

Together with the work of Russell and *The Times* there was, in the Crimea, another new development in what is now called the media, the introduction of photography. This was due, in the first place, to an Englishman named Roger Fenton, who arrived in the war zone with a horse-drawn van which served him as studio, dark room, store room and living quarters. Somewhat surprisingly Fenton, in contrast with Russell, was immediately on the best of terms with the whole army, from Raglan down. According to Fenton himself, this was due, at least as far as the junior officers and other ranks were concerned, to the novelty of photography and a general desire of almost everyone concerned to have their pictures taken.

News reporting, photography, telegraphy, and embryonic medical services were to make the war in the Crimea the first of the 'modern' wars. Generals were no longer just leaders of men, but managers of vast and complex politico-military machines, which were to come into their own in the twentieth century.

Guns with explosive shells instead of round shot, and rifles with increased accuracy and rapidity of fire entered into mass production, and effectively meant the end of wooden warships and serried ranks of brightly dressed soldiery.

Only fourteen years before the Crimea the British army abandoned the famous 'Brown Bess', a muzzle-loading, smooth-bore musket, which had had a life of 150 years. Its range was from 100 to 150 yards and its rate of fire three rounds a minute when used by the army and five to seven rounds when used by the more highly trained Royal Marines. This rate of fire compares with the famous standard of fifteen aimed rounds a minute maintained by the British

Expeditionary Force in 1914. The British rate of fire was one which could only be maintained by a highly trained, long-service force, but all the other armies of the world also advanced, as the British had done, from muzzle-loading smooth-bore muskets to the introduction of rifling which improved both the range and the aim, and then to breech-loading rifles with magazines containing between five or ten rounds.

Over a century after its adoption the Brown Bess was still not popular, and one senior officer made out a very convincing case for the use of the long bow on the grounds that it was more accurate than a musket, had four times the rate of fire and did not discharge smoke which could conceal the target and reveal the fire, while 'a flight of arrows coming upon them terrifies and disturbs the enemy's attention to his business', and, finally, 'bows and arrows were more easily made than muskets and ammunition'.

From 1859 onwards, during two decades, French, Russian, Italian, Austrian, Turkish, Danish and Prussian armies, as well as those of the Balkans and of minor German states, fought seven wars in Europe and re-drew the map of the Continent.

Hardly realized at the time, however, was the fact that the practice of the art of war was given a much greater impetus from events in the Civil War in America than from the dozen or so wars which took place on the other continents, for the American war gave a preview of developments some fifty years ahead. There were mass armies — three million men mobilized and supplied by the two sides out of a total population of thirty-six million; industry was organized for war production, railways were used to move and supply troops and this, together with the enormous growth in the power of small arms, produced circumstances which, apart from the changes wrought by the internal combustion engine, raised the rival armies close to the technical level of those of 1914. They were even ahead of 1914 in at least one respect, for they learned the vital need of digging in on the battlefield. The rifle pits of the Civil War were the trenches and foxholes of the two World Wars.

All this cost the two sides combined one million dead, a higher proportion of dead to total population than that suffered by Britain in the First World War. It should, however, be remembered that more than half the fatal casualties in the Civil War and, indeed, in nearly all great campaigns prior to 1914, were the result of disease rather than of enemy action.

Within a few months of the end of the Civil War the huge modern and experienced American armies had been swept away. Compulsory military service ('the draft') was abolished in the United States for the next half century and the war and its lessons disappeared from the minds of most European soldiers, apart from a few historians, of whom the best known was Colonel G. F. H. Henderson of the British army, author of the classic *Stonewall Jackson and the American Civil War*.

After the Prussian wars with Denmark, Austria and France between 1864 and 1871, and the Russo-Turkish War of 1877-8, the

Treaty of Berlin brought something of détente amongst the European powers, despite a series of cliff-hanging confrontations which continued until the final catastrophe in 1914. In the series of crises which had preceded the peace cobbled together in Berlin in 1878 the great European powers had all come close enough to war to be temporarily frightened of pushing to extremes, but no peace settlement outlives the generation that makes it and in 1908 rivalry between Austria and Russia wrecked the Treaty of Berlin.

The thirty years leading up to 1908 were comparatively peaceful although the development of weapons of war proceeded rapidly. This lull led to a profound lack of appreciation of the destructiveness of these new weapons which was really beyond comprehension. Perfected now was a gun which was capable of continuous rapid mechanical fire, and it was this weapon, more than any other, which was to lead to the mass slaughter and stalemate of the First World War. In its earliest form, this gun was known by the French as the mitrailleuse.

To maintain a high rate of fire it was equipped with twenty-five barrels; the Gatling and the Nordenfeldt, both famous early machine guns, also had multiple barrels but the machine guns which have since become standard weapons have single barrels and derive their rapidity of fire from the force of their recoil, which ejects the spent cartridge and replaces it in the breech by a fresh round at a rate approaching 600 rounds a minute, although no gun could, or would need to, produce such a rate of fire for more than a few seconds at a time.

When it came to the final test of war the place of the machine gun as compared to the rifle was clearly defined in the phrase quoted by all machine-gun instructors in the British army: 'Saul has slain his thousands and David his tens of thousands.'

Up to the middle of the nineteenth century and for a few years afterwards the position of the artillery in battle had been in front or on the flanks of its own infantry, from where it could blast away at the enemy, without his short-range hostile small arms being able to reach it in reply. Napoleon, himself a gunner, relied heavily on these tactics which, on a vastly greater scale, were to be copied in the artillery bombardments of the First World War.

Previously, when a gun was fired it ran backwards under the impetus of its recoil, and then had to be laboriously manhandled back to its firing position. But quick-firing guns absorbed their own shock of recoil by means of obturators, and remained in position ready for the next round. An additional advantage was that the gun crew, instead of standing aside when the gun crashed back, could remain protected by the shield with which field and the lighter horse artillery guns were henceforward fitted.

In the development of the quick-firing field gun the French army took a lead and the 75 millimetre gun was another of the 'secret weapons' which have flourished since the days when the industrial revolution first began to impinge upon the manufacture of arms. It was details of the '75' which Dreyfus was accused of supplying to

Germany in the famous spy case of the 1890s.

The development of artillery was matched by that of infantry and although the way in which the two arms were employed changed, their vital importance remained. On the other hand, the value of cavalry as a battlefield arm was much reduced. Instead of an arm which, massively committed, could decide a battle in a great charge, cavalry in the face of rifle fire had become simply a scouting arm. But before the *arme blanche* and the legends which surrounded it finally disappeared, it was to achieve a final success in battle in August 1870 during the fighting around Metz in an action which was perhaps the last successful cavalry charge in Western European warfare.

On 16 August 1870, the Franco-Prussian War being a month and a day old, Marshal Bazaine was leading his army, 160,000 strong, out of Metz, falling back to join the rest of the French army under Napoleon. From Metz westward there were four different roads which could have been taken by Bazaine but, for some reason not understood to this day, he used only one of them, with the result that his army formed a column so long that it took two days and nights to pass a given point. In hot pursuit Alvensleben's Third Corps encountered a French force west of Metz, watering its horses amidst pitched tents; the Germans believed that they had found the tail of the retreating army. Instead Alvensleben found that he had overtaken the entire French army, which was now between his corps and the main body of the German army. The only way in which Alvensleben could deter the French from launching an attack of overwhelming strength upon him was to give the French the impression that they had the whole German army before them. To carry out this bold plan Alvensleben had available only two regiments of cavalry, each of three squadrons, a total of 800 men, commanded by General von Bredow, who at once led his men into battle, with their objective a line of French guns established between Rezonville and Vionville. The charge was so unexpected, and was carried out with such dash, that the German cavalry passed through the French infantry with few casualties and dashed on, only to be attacked from the rear by the French infantrymen as they recovered from their surprise. French cavalry then joined in from a flank and swirling groups of horsemen fought it out, with flashing sabres, until what was left of the Germans withdrew. They were only half of the total number that had charged but they had done their work. The fall back of the French was stopped and Bazaine withdrew into Metz where he was besieged and eventually compelled to surrender on 27 October. The charge became famous in German military history as 'Bredow's Death Ride'.

Paris, in the meanwhile, was sustaining its own siege from 20 September 1870 until 28 January 1871. An armistice followed three days later and peace was proclaimed on 1 March. War between the nations of Western Europe was at an end for forty-three years.

In south-eastern Europe the efforts of the Balkan nations to free themselves, under Russian auspices, from Turkish rule led to a series of wars in which the Balkan peoples not only fought the Turks but also, from time to time, each other.

In 1876 Serbia attacked Turkey, was defeated and had to be rescued by Russia in the following year; Romania and Bulgaria attached themselves to the Russian army, which fought its way to the lines of Chataldja in the suburbs of Constantinople. This war ended with the Treaty of Berlin in 1878.

Seven years later Serbia again attacked a neighbouring state, this time Bulgaria; disastrous results followed and the European powers were obliged to come to her rescue, after her army had sustained a fortnight of defeat. This was the war which is the background of G. B. Shaw's *Arms and the Man* and of *The Chocolate Soldier*. Its most important feature was the demonstration which it gave of the powers of endurance possessed by Balkan troops. In this case it was the Bulgarian infantry units who, in the middle of a Balkan winter, marched through the mountains, covering fifty-nine miles in thirty-two hours, but Serbians, Greeks, Montenegrans and Turks were later to show the same characteristics. During their advance, one Bulgarian battalion moved on horseback, two men to a horse, while other units travelled by rail, sixty men to a small open goods wagon.

In 1897 the Greeks made an unsuccessful attack on the Turks and they, in turn, had to be rescued by the powers who, however, awarded them the historic Greek province of Thessaly and in 1912-13 the First and Second Balkan Wars left Turkey in Europe confined to the bridgehead covering Constantinople and the Dardanelles, where the Turkish frontier now lies.

By the middle of the nineteenth century the peoples of Latin America had won their independence after a series of armed struggles, but they were unable to settle down to unchecked peaceful development. A succession of civil wars, revolutions, coups d'état and pronunciamentos, though usually carried out bloodlessly or with small loss of life, severely hampered the advance of these new nations. There were, however, also several fully-fledged wars, civil or international, a series which began, as far as the latter half of the century was concerned, with the Mexican Civil War of 1858-61, followed by the intervention of the French in support of Napoleon III's dream of an American empire. Once the American Civil War was at an end the United States threatened to intervene, and the French withdrew.

In 1864 there began a war which, from the point of view of the casualties suffered by one of the belligerents and the damage done to their country, ranks as one of the most horrible in the history of warfare in 'civilized' times. Francisco Lopez, having succeeded his father as dictator of Paraguay, then a country with a population of little more than a million, decided to make a bid for the status of a major Latin American power. In doing so he found himself at war simultaneously with Brazil, Argentina and Uruguay. The war lasted for five years, at the end of which the population of Paraguay had been reduced from 1,300,000 to 220,000, only 28,000 of whom were men above the age of fifteen. Boys between twelve and fifteen years old had also been conscripted to form entire units. Women were forced to carry stores and ammunition until they fell exhausted, when they were either abandoned to die or killed on the spot by their own troops.

When the war was clearly lost, Lopez issued orders that foreshadowed those of Hitler in similar circumstances; as the Paraguayans retreated they were systematically to destroy every building they passed and slaughter every animal that they could not take with them. These orders were carried out. Finally, driven northward, the Paraguayans made a final stand at the Aquidaban River where, on 1 May 1870, they were completely defeated and Lopez killed.

War between Latin American nations ceased east of the Andes until the Chaco struggle between Bolivia and Paraguay which lasted from 1932 to 1935. On the Pacific coast the ambitions and troubles of Chile led to two more wars. First, from 1879 to 1884, there was fought what was known as the Great Pacific War. Chile, Bolivia and Peru disputed the right to exploit the nitrate fields which lay mainly in the Bolivian coastal province of Atacama. There were scanty communications by land, so that the course of the war depended on command of the sea. Here at first the advantage lay with the Peruvians, possessors of the most powerful warships in the Pacific, but once these ships had been put out of action, Chilean troop movements could proceed almost unchecked. The Bolivians were expelled from their coastal districts and the nitrate fields. The Chileans advanced into Peru and succeeded in capturing the capital city of Lima. Peace was not finally signed until April 1884.

Chile was again at war in 1891 when a rebellion broke out under circumstances which were to be closely paralleled by the events of 1973. A left-wing president, José Balmaceda, found himself at odds with a right-wing Congress. War developed in a way which would have provided a first-class scenario for a simple war-game, the army supporting the President while the navy followed its senior officers and Congress. The President began to gather a small but adequate fleet in France to sail to Chile and overcome the Congressionalists who, in the meantime, had collected an army which was brought south by sea to attack Valparaiso and Santiago, and this force was able to take both towns before the rescuing Balmacedist fleet arrived.

*   *   *   *

Throughout the second half of the nineteenth century there was a continuous series of colonial wars in which British, Indian, German, French, Italian, Spanish, Japanese, and, from 1898, American troops were engaged. Both Russia and America were simultaneously clearing their territories of their indigenous populations. Britain's small all-volunteer force had been built up for just this role, while in Europe public opinion was against sending conscripts to fight abroad. As a result, the colonial powers had to form long-term volunteer forces like the French Foreign Legion.

These colonial wars were also responsible for the fact that the appearance of almost all the armies of the world began to change. In the campaigns on the Indian frontier the red tunics of the British troops were frighteningly conspicuous, while the khaki of the Indians melted into the background. Accordingly, the use of khaki by British troops spread from India to Egypt and the Sudan and then to South Africa, so that the British red coat, except for ceremonial occasions, disappeared in 1902. Eventually the American, Japanese and Russian armies all adopted various shades of khaki. But it was not until 1915, one year after the beginning of the First World War, that the last of the colourful and totally impractical uniforms of the previous century were finally replaced. The Germans adopted field grey in 1910, the Austrians pike grey in 1909, and then field grey in 1915. In 1915 the French finally introduced horizon blue, and the Italians grey-green.

Probably one of the oldest military customs is the emulation of the victorious. During the second half of the nineteenth century French military prestige was so high that many old-established and newly-formed armies adopted French uniforms (for example the Italians, both armies during the American Civil War, the Scandinavians, and the Japanese). Distinctive features of the French style were the képi with bands of metallic lace denoting rank, dark blue or almost black tunics with lace or frogging, and rank distinctions on the cuffs formed from elaborate knots of gold braid. German uniforms were also much admired and even copied by the British, who, according to Liddell Hart, not only adopted the Prussian spiked helmet but its contents as well.

Even in civilian life there were many foreigners who slavishly copied English tastes and customs, and so it was not surprising that the experience in matters of dress gained by the British in sport and battle in the far-flung empire, was also copied. From India came the muddy colour called khaki, the sun helmet, the strips of cloth which were bound round the legs, the Sam Browne belt, and many other bits of pseudo-functionalism. By the 1920s these innovations had been so widely copied, that there was only an occasional 'old-fashioned' army dressed in anything but khaki or one of its derivatives.

At the same time as changes were being made in the appearance and equipment of the principal armies of the world, radical changes were also being made in the methods by which they were recruited, and hence in the type of men who comprised them, their standard of training and the kind of war they fought. The great victories of the French Revolution and the Empire had been won by armies raised by conscription. Once Napoleon was safely installed on St Helena, however, there was a general desire in France to get rid of all Napoleonic practices, and as early as 1848 a new system was introduced. Recruits were still to be selected by the drawing of lots but, as the men called up were only a proportion of those available, it was easy for the unlucky in the draw to buy a substitute, if they possessed the means. These substitutes, who would take their place for the statutory period of seven years, were obviously among the poorest members of the community and tended to become professional soldiers since they were seldom able to become skilled in any civilian trade while serving in the ranks and they had little alternative to re-enlistment. This system of recruiting paved the way for the French disasters of 1870.

The Prussians who, after Jena, had owed their recovery to Scharnhorst's introduction of conscription, also allowed their system of recruiting to collapse. This resulted in the Austrians obtaining a great diplomatic success over the Prussians under an agreement called 'The Punctuation of Ölmütz' in 1850. After the troubles in 1848-9, Prussia had decided to challenge Austria for the leadership of the German states, but when the confrontation took place it was clear to the Prussians that their army was in no state to match the Austrians. They accordingly gave way and the Austrians obtained a diplomatic supremacy over the German states which lasted for fifteen years. One result of this was that the Prussians were discouraged from joining in the Crimean War on the side of the allies. At the same time, the leaders in Berlin began to manoeuvre in the parliament for the credits necessary to rebuild the army.

When the principal powers began to digest the lessons of the Crimean War it became clear to them all that their armies were in need of great reorganization. For all armies, except those of Britain and the United States, this meant the introduction of systems of compulsory military service which were, in theory at least, universal. Every citizen was obliged to spend a period, usually of two or three years, in the army on reaching the age of twenty or twenty-one. When that period was over the conscript went back to civil life as a member of the reserve and, as such, returned to the army every few years for re-training, and remained liable to recall in the event of mobilization. This system, which came to be regarded by those to whom it applied as as much a fact of life as the payment of taxes, was the only way in which the nations could maintain the large armies which they felt necessary, for they could not afford to pay their soldiers on a scale which would have provided a living wage for a single man, let alone one with a wife and children. Only Britain and the United States felt able to do without large conscript armies — the United States being sufficiently far from Europe, the British trusting in their navy to protect them from invasion.

From 1854 to 1914, the rate of those developments which were just beginning after the battle of the Alma, grew and gathered speed and the experiences of particular countries led to the re-casting of war on a different and much larger scale. In the course of those years, in half-forgotten battles over different terrains, and after numberless peace treaties, what all nations had learned went into the change in the appearance, conduct, and causes of the armies preparing to fight the First World War.

I·CONSCRIPT ARMIES OF EUROPE

1 PRUSSIA & GERMANY

Above: Prussian riflemen (Jäger) demonstrate their tactics when approaching an enemy. Scouts, protected by an advance party, observe enemy movements. The company commander conveys his orders via the bugler, while an orderly holds his horse. The company waits in the rear for the signal to move forward.

The last half century of European history before the outbreak of the First World War was dominated by the German army. Three short, sharp, victorious wars between 1864 and 1871 not only transformed it from a collection of armies of different values belonging to the various German states into the most formidable army that Europe had seen since Napoleon, but also united those states into a great power.

Yet in 1849, only fifteen years previously, Prussia had been thwarted in her attempts to seize the duchy of Holstein by Austria with her Swedish, Norwegian, Danish, Saxon and Hanoverian allies, and the discreet presence of the British Royal Navy. In 1850 at the Treaty of Ölmütz Prussia was made to feel a very second-rate power and was forced to abstain from her efforts to assume leadership of a united Germany.

Prussian mobilization at the time of the Ölmütz crisis had taken six weeks. Untrained reservists reported to their depots with no uniforms and antique weapons. It had been hoped to make use of railways for the first time in the deployment of troops, but the railwaymen had been called up to serve as infantry, cavalry or artillery so there was no one left to man the trains. This was especially disastrous as the army had no horse-drawn transport of its own. These shortcomings were symptomatic of the generally lack-lustre spirit which pervaded the Prussian army at this time. The meticulous performance of formal exercises on the parade ground seemed the be-all and end-all of military preparation. Most other armies at this time suffered similarly but the Prussians seem to have adopted this attitude with a peculiar intensity. It was not until the appointment of Moltke as Chief of Staff in 1857 that matters began their extraordinarily rapid improvement.

To re-establish the prestige of Prussia and her army there followed a seven-year struggle between the government and parliament, with the latter jealous of its powers, hostile to the army, and generally unwilling to vote the money which it required. By 1864, however, Bismarck recognized that the people were opposed to war but he believed that an early victory would swing public opinion behind his policy, which he could then continue to pursue unchecked. So it was that between 1864 and 1871 the Prussian army and Bismarck turned Europe upside down. Of the big powers only Britain and Russia were not immediately affected by the changes brought about when, after a quasi-civil war in 1866 between the German states lasting only seven weeks, Prussia welded the component parts of Germany into the strongest state of continental Europe. Moreover, thanks to the new Germany, the kingdom of Italy was consolidated, while Austria-Hungary and France suffered important losses of territory and, even more vital, losses of power and prestige to the benefit of Germany.

For more than four hundred years the question of Schleswig-Holstein had lain in the vaults of European history, breeding complications on such a scale that when Palmerston, the British Prime Minister, was called upon to grapple with it in 1864 he

Left: Frederick, Prince of Prussia (later Frederick III and father of the last Kaiser, William II), inspects one of his infantrymen, c. 1858.

announced that it had been understood by only three people in history; the Prince Consort, who was dead, a Danish minister who had gone mad, and Palmerston himself, who had forgotten the answer. The complications and remoteness of the affair may be judged by the fact that a large part of its background rested upon the Salic Law, which forbade inheritance of territory through the female line.

The series of incidents which brought about the changes in the Prussian army began with the re-appearance of the Schleswig-Holstein problem in 1864. Frederick VII of Denmark, who died in 1863, had held the duchies of Schleswig and Holstein separately from the Danish crown. The succession to the Danish crown ran through the female line, but succession through the female line was forbidden in the duchies, where the Duke of Augustenberg, presented as the legitimate claimant by Prussia and Austria, was opposed by the Danes.

In support of their candidate Austria and Prussia, under the Prussian Field-Marshal von Wrangel, invaded Holstein on 1 February 1864. The Austrians headed directly north towards Jutland, while the Prussians turned right opposite the island of Alsen. At Düppel, a strong bridgehead had been formed by the Danes, covering the approaches to the island, and providing a position from which their forces could be concentrated for a sortie against the Austro-Prussian lines of communication.

The Düppel lines were stormed by the Prussians on 18 April, with 1200 killed and wounded. The Danes suffered almost the same losses in killed and wounded but also lost 5000 prisoners. As Bismarck had foreseen, the Prussian success had an immediate effect on the morale of the home front, which became enthusiastic in support of Bismarck's policy of aggression. The Austro-Prussian advance continued until all but the northernmost tip of Jutland was in their hands. By then the great powers, who had been continuing their pre-war efforts at mediation, succeeded in arranging an armistice. A conference began in London on 12 May 1864 and lasted until 25 June, when negotiations broke down and the war was briefly resumed, finally ending on 1 August. Austria and Prussia quarrelled over the division of the spoils, and both Schleswig and Holstein were annexed by Prussia.

Bismarck proceeded to instigate another war, this time against his former ally Austria. An early step in preparation for this had been the conclusion of an alliance between Prussia and Italy, so that when war came an important part of the Austrian army would be diverted from Prussia to cope with the Italians to the south. As a reward for this service, Bismarck promised the Italians that they should have Venice as soon as the war was won. Bismarck's design was to usurp Austria's influence amongst the German states. This he successfully did as soon as his diplomatic preparations with Italy were complete.

It was easy enough to pick a quarrel with Austria over the future of Schleswig and Holstein. During the spring of 1866 both Prussia and Austria mobilized while Austria appealed to the other German states for assistance. Prussia then unilaterally denounced her Confederation with Austria and invaded Saxony on 15 June, without a declaration of war.

There followed three short campaigns. In the north, Prussian territory was divided into two parts, separated by Hanover, and the Prussians' first concern was to close this gap. This was done, but only after the Prussians had been defeated by the Hanoverians at Langensalza on 27 June.

On 20 June Italy had declared war on Austria, and, four days later, her troops crossed what was then the Austrian border at Peschiera and Custozza near Verona. The Italian army, nominally commanded by King Victor Emmanuel II, with La Marmora, his Chief of Staff, in actual command, numbered 100,000, while the Austrian forces under Archduke Albrecht totalled 73,000. The Italians were repulsed in confusion and the reason for hostilities

Opposite: Prussian troops in Broager during the Prussian-Danish War in 1864.

between Austria and Italy ceased to exist on 3 July, when the Austrian Emperor Francis Joseph agreed to surrender Venetia.

On the same day that Francis Joseph handed over Venetia, the decisive battle of the war was fought between the Prussians and Austrians in Bohemia. By the beginning of July three Prussian armies, with Moltke exercising supreme command under the titular leadership of King William of Prussia, had gathered for the invasion of the Austrian Empire. The First Army (under Prince Frederick Charles) and the Army of the Elbe (under General von Bittenfeld) were to advance south-eastward from Saxony (already overrun by the Prussians) and the Second Army (under the Crown Prince, afterwards Kaiser Frederick III) was to advance southward from Silesia. Benedek, the Austrian commander-in-chief, met them between Königgrätz and Sadowa, from which places the battle takes its two names. Benedek's army was 205,000 strong (including a Saxon corps of 23,000) while the combined Prussian armies totalled 300,000.

A daring reconnaissance by a single Prussian officer revealed the Austrian position and Moltke drafted his orders for the First and Elbe armies to attack head on, while the Second Army came in on the Austrian right flank. By the end of the day the Prussians had lost 9000 men but the Austrian and Saxon casualties were 40,000, and the Austrian resistance was at an end.

From the technical point of view the Prussian victory had been due to the superiority of their breech-loading rifle (the Dreyse Needle-Gun) over the muzzle-loaders of the Austrians. Although the Austrian Lorenz had a longer range than the needle-gun, the latter could be loaded by a man lying down, while it was necessary to stand up to load the Lorenz through its muzzle.

The Seven Weeks War ended on 20 August 1866. Prussia became master of north Germany, Austria was deprived of her commanding position in German affairs, and the scene was set for Bismarck's third war. Prussia's victory over Austria led almost fatally to the war against France. The success of Bismarck's policy had been watched anxiously by Napoleon, who saw his personal prestige, and that of France, eroded rapidly when he failed to gain the compensation in Belgium or on the left bank of the Rhine which he believed necessary to preserve the balance between France and Prussia.

Accordingly, Napoleon began dilatory and vague negotiations for alliances with both Italy and Austria. These had achieved no results when, suddenly, there threatened another victory, bloodless this time, for Prussia. The vacant throne of Spain was offered to Prince Leopold of Hohenzollern-Sigmaringen, a cousin of the King of Prussia. The French reaction to the possibility of a hostile Spain to the south, as well as a hostile Prussia to the east, was predictably violent, but Napoleon, to begin with, extracted a diplomatic success from the incident. Prince Leopold's father, anticipating trouble, forbade him to accept the throne. On the other hand Bismarck wanted, if not war, at least a further humiliation for France. This he

Right: Frederick III, who became German Emperor in 1888, but reigned for only 88 days.

Below: Field-Marshal Graf von Moltke, the brilliant Prussian military reformer, c. 1880.

Below right: In 1884 Bismarck arranged the 'three Kaiser pact' in an attempt to settle the differences which beset the great European powers. From left to right: Russian Foreign Minister von Giers, Reich Chancellor von Bismarck, and Austro-Hungarian Foreign Minister Graf Kalnoky, at Czernowitz, September 1884.

obtained by judicious sub-editing of the famous Ems telegram, to give the impression that the Prussian King had been insulted and that war would follow, which it did, being declared by France against Prussia on 19 July 1870.

The course of this war depended to an even greater extent than usual upon the equipment and organization of the rival armies. The armies of Prussia and the German states, which had been her enemies in 1866, were formed by conscription. Until 1868 the French army had been recruited on what was virtually a voluntary basis, and the change to compulsory service had only been half completed; its reserves, such as they were, were hardly organized. On the other hand, the French rifle, the chassepot, and the mitrailleuse gave it advantages which the Germans did not possess. The German artillery, thanks largely to Krupp, was better than the French, but it was the superiority of the German staff work which was to ensure German success.

Originally, the French had planned an immediate invasion of southern Germany and a link-up with the Austrians in Bavaria, followed by a joint advance on Berlin. The speed of the Prussian advance, however, made it clear to Austria and Italy that they would be defeated once again if they declared war and, accordingly, they remained neutral.

On the Franco-German frontier in Lorraine one of the two main

At the victorious conclusion of the Franco-Prussian War, the German Reich was proclaimed in the Galerie des Glaces at Versailles on 18 January 1871. Here Bismarck was photographed among staff officers and foreign office officials.

French armies, that of the Rhine, formed up 200,000 strong, while the other army, that of Châlons of about half that size, was assembling belatedly at Châlons-sur-Marne. The Germans, again under the nominal command of their King but actually under that of Moltke, drove the Army of the Rhine, commanded by Marshal Bazaine, back into Metz and in a series of fierce battles prevented them from escaping.

Meanwhile the Army of Châlons, with Napoleon III in nominal, but with Marshal MacMahon in actual, command, started to the rescue of Metz. Intercepted by Moltke at Sedan, the army was surrounded and forced to surrender, Napoleon going with his troops into captivity.

With the two main French armies thus accounted for there was nothing to hinder the Prussian advance on Paris. The city was encircled and besieged from 20 September 1870 to 28 January 1871, while to protect the besieging army the Prussians extended their hold over nearly all of France north of the Loire. After an armistice, France finally surrendered on 26 February. Alsace and part of Lorraine were annexed by Prussia, who also received a huge indemnity of five thousand million gold francs (about £240 million at that time).

Paris was then to pass through an even more terrible ordeal than the siege — the Commune and its sequel. The Prussians went home victorious, having proclaimed the King of Prussia German Emperor in the Galerie des Glaces in the Palace of Versailles where, forty-eight years later, the peace treaty which ended the First World War was signed. The German army returned to a welcome so enthusiastic that its commanders were able to consolidate a position in the state which gave them the status of a parallel government side by side with the civil power, a form of control that has never worked. In Germany before 1914, the two halves of the state, military and civil, competed with each other and the main cause of contention was finance. The amount of money voted to the army limited its strength, and in 1874 the Reichstag (the parliament of the new German Empire) was asked to agree to a total strength of 400,000 men, fixed by law and unalterable by parliament for a period of seven years. The force was placed under the supreme command of the Kaiser, as William I had now become, except the Bavarian Army (three army corps) which would be under the King of Bavaria and administered by the Bavarian ministry of war in peace-time, though reverting to the control of Berlin in time of war. The Württemberg Army (one army corps) had its officers appointed by the King of Württemberg, although in peace and war it was commanded by the Kaiser. There was no Reich War Minister since that authority was exercised by the Prussian War Minister.

As if disputes between the army and the Reichstag were not trouble enough, a reorganization of the highest levels of the army itself, carried out in 1883, made the Ministry of War, the General Staff, and the Kaiser's military cabinet, mutually independent agencies. The fact that the naval high command was organized as the same kind of three-headed monster meant that all six heads competed with each other, fought the Kaiser, and battled with the Reichstag as well, thus causing a continual state of turmoil and disputes at the higher levels of government when it came to the allocation of funds. Until the late 1890s the lion's share of available money went to the army, but once Tirpitz convinced the Kaiser of the need for a strong navy it was clear there would not be enough money for everything that both the army and navy claimed they required. In 1895 the army cut the period of military service from three to two years, in consequence.

Shortage of money and the demands of the navy meant that Germany could only call up annually in peace-time half the number of men fit for service, while the French called up everyone. On the other hand, in 1914 in the opening days of the war, Germany mobilized eighty-seven divisions and France sixty-two, the startling discrepancy being due to the fact that, to the surprise of all foreign experts, the Germans were able to use reserve divisions whose number virtually duplicated the peace-time strength. The German ability to do this was a kind of secret weapon in their possession which, in the first month of the war, enabled them to outflank the French and British forces and almost encircle them. Had this encirclement succeeded it would have ended the war on land in the same way that the three victorious wars fought by Prussia had ended in 1864, 1866 and 1871. To the Germans in 1914 there seemed

Below: Prussian Guards officers at their annual autumn parade on the Tempelhoferfeld, Berlin on 1 September 1910.

General Graf von Schlieffen, Chief of the General Staff of the German army from 1891 to 1905.

no reason why history should not repeat itself, and then the German army could turn eastward and deal with the Russians. Once the British had been driven out of the Continent, they would be only too glad to settle on moderate terms. Although the Germans had created the finest army in the world, and laid most carefully detailed plans for its use in war, they also made colossal errors in the planning of its prelude and these were to make victory impossible.

The master plan for the German army had been devised by Schlieffen, Chief of the Great General Staff from 1891 until 1906, and its execution demanded two potentially disastrous preconditions. In the first place, the plan was based on the idea of war with both France and Russia, and although the immediate aim of the Germans in 1914 was to prevent, by threat of war or war itself, the Russians from attacking Austria, it was necessary for the German plan to involve France. Accordingly an ultimatum was addressed to Paris demanding that, as a guarantee of neutrality, the French fortresses of Toul and Verdun should be handed over. It was appreciated that the demand would be refused, but the refusal would provide the pretext for war which the Germans sought.

The second condition called for the invasion of Belgium which led directly to the entry into war of Britain. The failure to provide flexibility in the German plan was a fatal mistake which was copied by the French in the years between the First and Second World Wars.

Pre-military training for school children in Prussia, 1912.

29

PRUSSIA & GERMANY

History and traditions The fighting traditions of
the Prussian army were forged under the leadership
of two men: Frederick William I, the
'Sergeant-King', who reigned from 1713 to 1740, and
his son Frederick the Great. The military vacuum
created by the death of Frederick in 1786 was finally
filled during the Napoleonic Wars by the reforming
combination of Scharnhorst, Grolman, Gneisenau
and Clausewitz. Under their patronage the
Federfuchsern (progressive activists) were able to
lay the foundations of the German army of 1914
despite the entrenched opposition of the
Federbuschen (traditionalists). Of the men and
institutions which worked to perfect the Prussian
army none was more influential than the Great
General Staff. Formed under Grolman in 1817, this
new organization was the motive force behind all
military preparation for war, and once hostilities had
begun it assumed responsibility for their conduct.
The army's commitment to national policies coupled
with the revenge it gained over France in 1870-1 for
the Napoleonic humiliation of defeat and occupation,
welded a unique bond of loyalty and respect between
soldier and civilian. The strength of the bond, which
had been actively fostered by Germany's leaders,
was shown in 1914 when the nation went to war with
an unequalled belief in their country's destiny and in
the army as an instrument of victory.

Strength With a German population in 1910 of 66.4
million, the army could draw upon considerable
reserves of manpower for service in war. The peace
establishment of the army at 545,000 men was lower
than that of both France and Russia, but in 1900 the
number of enrolled men for war was set at 6,213,000.
This enormous total was composed of an offensive
force of 3,013,000 men and a Landsturm of 3,200,000.

System of recruiting An army corps was allocated
to each of the nineteen military districts of Germany
and recruits were enrolled in the corps stationed in
their home areas. The number of recruits required
each year was assessed, on advice from the army, by
the Emperor who then apportioned the total
requirement according to the population of each state.

Terms of service The principle of compulsory
service was established by law on 3 September 1814,
and it continued in force until 1919. The liability for
service spanned a period of twenty-seven years from
the age of seventeen to forty-five, and it was divided
into active service and Landsturm service. Each man
was called up at twenty, served either two years in
the infantry or three years in the cavalry and horse
artillery, four or five years in its reserve, then eleven
years in the Landwehr and finally seven in the
Landsturm. The Landsturm also contained men
between the ages of seventeen and twenty who had
not yet served, while recruits who had been excused
active service due to special exemption for medical

*Crown Prince William of Prussia
in the undress uniform of
the 1st Life Hussar Regiment.*

*Kaiser William II in the
uniform of the Mounted Rifles
(Jäger zu Pferde), c. 1911.*

Above: The Kaiserin with her six sons, from left to right:
Oscar, Eitel-Frederick, William, Adalbert, Joachim and Augustus William.
Below: Prussian reservists pose outside their barracks, c. 1911.

reasons were allocated to the Ersatz Reserve. For young men of education and substance the period of service in the active army was reduced to one year, but they were required to provide their own food, equipment, uniform, and where necessary, horses. Men who sought a career of active service could volunteer for two, three or four years, and then re-engage. The majority of NCOs were drawn from this category.

Officers Entry to the officer corps was either through attendance at a cadet school or through acceptance as an Avantageur. The Avantageurs were required to pass a special examination or gain exemption by diploma, to serve five months as privates, and gain a certificate of military competence by the age of twenty-three. Cadets were trained from the age of eleven in one of ten cadet schools, passing at the age of fifteen to the Lichterfelde Academy near Berlin. Before commissioning, both classes of officer recruits were required to complete a thirty-five-week course at one of the army's eleven war schools.

Organization The army was organized into five separate categories when placed on a war footing. The active army brought up to strength by its reserves represented the first category, while the second comprised the field reserve troops formed from men not required by the active army on mobilization. The Landwehr formed the third category and it was charged with the defence of fortresses and lines of communication. The fourth consisted of the depot troops and the fifth of the Landsturm.

Infantry The infantry comprised 175 regiments, each consisting of three battalions of four companies. In addition a Jäger battalion was attached to each army corps. Both the infantry and the cavalry of the German army were drawn from the national contingents of Prussia, Saxony, Württemberg, and Bavaria. With the exception of those from Bavaria all infantry regiments were given two numbers, one representing their order in the German army and the other their order in their national army.

Infantry hold a line of trenches against an attack by the cavalry. Even at the height of the folly of the First World War, such senseless manoeuvres were not carried out. Kaiser manoeuvres in Silesia, 1913.

Cavalry The cavalry consisted of ninety-three regiments of which seventy-three were provided by Prussia, ten by Bavaria, six by Saxony and four by Württemberg. Each regiment contained five squadrons with a combined mobilization strength of twenty-three officers and 602 men. The total cavalry establishment was second in size only to that of Russia. The Uhlans were light cavalry armed with a lance and straight sword, and with the battlefield tasks of reconnaissance and security.

Artillery The artillery was divided into two branches: the field and horse artillery and the foot or garrison artillery. The former consisted of forty-three regiments, the latter of seventeen regiments.

Engineers The technical branch of the army was composed of twenty-three pioneer battalions, three regiments and one battalion of railway troops, and two balloon detachments.

Among European armies, the Germans were alone in recognizing the extent to which an effective military machine could be quickly formed from short-service levies commanded by a thoroughly trained cadre of officers and NCOs. Their exploitation of this capacity in 1914, by using reserve divisions as front-line troops from mobilization, nullified the French plan of campaign at a stroke. By the end of the nineteenth century the German army was seen, in terms of leadership, equipment, and military institutions, as the premier fighting force in Europe, and its characteristics were copied by most of the world's armies. But there were weaknesses in this apparently flawless machine. There was, if anything, too much emphasis on the training and qualities of the individual officer, who was thereby often prompted to take crucial decisions on his own initiative in the belief that his view of a campaign or battle was the vital one. Despite their professionalism the Germans, like most other soldiers in Europe, failed to appreciate the changing nature of twentieth-century warfare until it burst upon them in 1914, by which time it was too late for radical rethinking.

Prussian Foot Guards, wearing field-grey uniforms, wait for an enemy attack in their entrenched positions, Kaiser manoeuvres, 1912.

Left: The Kaiser (second from left) and his staff during the 1913 manoeuvres in Silesia.

Right: The last summer of peace. Prussian officers at the races in Berlin, 1914.

Below: Prussian reservists carry a captured Russian colour to the Berlin Arsenal (Zeughaus), where it will be displayed with the other trophies of the victories in East Prussia, autumn 1914.

French Chasseurs d'Afrique in the Crimea, 1855. Their light blue jackets and red trousers were still being worn in 1914 (see the illustration on page 48). Below: The French army lands at Eupatoria in the Crimea, September 1854.

2 FRANCE

At the end of the 1850s the army of Napoleon III was such that it made the Emperor's ambition to rival his uncle seem by no means ridiculous. Thirty years of almost continuous fighting in North Africa and successful campaigns in the Crimea and northern Italy had gone, it was believed, to make an unequalled, long-service force. However, France's failure to secure the upper hand in the long drawn out Mexican campaign on behalf of the Emperor Maximilian, brother of Francis Joseph of Austria, (1861-7) lost her much prestige, and in 1868 a thoroughgoing overhaul of the whole military machine was begun. This followed the discovery, which had been made two years earlier, that while the total effective strength of the Prussian army with reserves was about 1,200,000 men, that of France was 288,000 including forces in Algeria, Mexico and Rome, where a contingent was protecting Papal territory from the newly-formed kingdom of Italy, which Napoleon III had helped to establish. Napoleon accordingly decided to increase his army to 1,000,000 by the introduction of compulsory military service, a measure which was attacked by the Right and the Left alike, the former led by senior army officers who still favoured a long-service professional force, while farm and factory workers alike objected to being conscripted.

Finally, in 1870, at the outbreak of the war with Prussia the army on a peace footing totalled 393,000 and, after the reserves had been called up, 567,000. This was just about half the strength of Prussia and the other German states, combined.

The balance of forces against the French was made worse by the defects of the French system of mobilization. Reservists called up for service with a specific unit very often found that that unit was many miles away; having completed what might well have been a long journey accompanied by delays inseparable from the traffic of mobilization they were then likely to discover that their unit had moved on to the area where it was to concentrate for war. German units, on the other hand, were made up of men who, in peace-time, lived and worked in the same area so that the actual process of joining a unit or mobilizing took hours rather than days. Arriving at their depot, troops would find their weapons, equipment, uniforms, and new boots awaiting them. A German from Hamburg who had been five years old in 1914 recalled, sixty years later, that his one memory of the great days when the troops marched through the town to entrain for the Front was the smell of thousands of pairs of new boots. French reservists, on the other hand, were issued with boots which they themselves had previously worn and broken in.

Liquid refreshment, and other services, were provided by women called 'cantinières', who used to dress in a female version of military uniform and accompany the troops on active service, 1855.

After the disasters at Sedan and Metz nearly half the French army was out of action, killed, wounded or prisoners, among the latter being Napoleon. With the two main French armies accounted for there was nothing between the Germans and Paris except a few straggling units totalling 60,000 men, facing an army of nearly one million. While the siege of Paris was in process, improvised French forces in the provinces made a series of attempts to relieve the capital, inspired by Léon Gambetta, who had escaped from Paris by balloon.

Bombardment and blockade brought about the French surrender and the end of the war. Alsace and part of Lorraine were annexed by Germany and a huge indemnity was paid.

Before the war there had already been a split developing between industrial workers in Paris and the peasants in the countryside who lived a life that was still traditional. During the war the people of Paris had fought themselves to a standstill, complaining that they had not been properly supported by the rest of France, which seemed to regard the war as a great inconvenience forced upon them by the capital. This split between Right and Left, countryside and capital city, had been made worse by the unruly, disorganized behaviour of the various official, semi-official and quite unofficial bodies which were the nearest approach that Paris had, during the siege, to a government.

Under the terms of the armistice the Germans had the right to occupy, for three days, the western part of Paris and on 1 March their troops marched under the Arc de Triomphe and down the Champs Elysées. To prevent some two hundred guns falling into the hands of the enemy the French authorities decided to collect them on the hill top of Montmartre, where the church of the Sacré Coeur now stands, and then remove them to safety. These guns belonged to the regular army, but the National Guard, originally recruited to protect law and order by the Conservative authorities, and now thoroughly permeated with left-wing extremism, decided that the regulars should not be permitted to take their guns away. In the chaos two generals were lynched by the crowd.

The National Guard and a provisional municipal government, which has gone down in history as the Commune, took over in Paris. The Germans withdrew to their occupation zone on the edge of the city and settled down to watch Frenchmen destroy each other. The legitimate government of France, which had withdrawn to Bordeaux during the siege, now moved to Versailles, and here the regular army was concentrated for the recapture of Paris. The Versailles forces took their time, but eventually began their counter-attack, preceded by heavy bombardments, during April. Altogether they were 130,000 strong, most of them, like their commander, Marshal MacMahon, former prisoners of the Germans who had been released from captivity for the work now in hand. They were spurred on by Bismarck himself, who told Thiers, acting head of the French government, that if they did not put down the Commune the Germans would.

A French horse artilleryman at the time of the war against Italy in 1859.

French artillery on the Buttes, Montmartre in Paris, 18 March 1871, just before the establishment of the Commune.

In Paris the various factions of the Commune intrigued against each other and the artillery of the Versailles troops drew closer day by day; the Communards built barricades mostly of paving stones, hostages were taken, of whom the most distinguished was the Archbishop of Paris, and preparations were made to destroy some of the most famous buildings in the city. On 21 May the Versailles troops broke into a Communard position, which had been left unguarded, and then fought their way into the city, street by street, and barricade by barricade. The Communards one by one executed their hostages, including the Archbishop. In all, some five hundred executions took place during the two months of the Commune. In the last days of the fighting the Imperial Palace of the Tuileries and the Hôtel de Ville were burned out by the Communards, and the Louvre nearly suffered the same fate.

The fighting in the city was ferocious and the Versailles troops gave little quarter, killing between 20,000 and 25,000 men and women. The outcome of this week's fighting has left a scar on French consciousness to this day.

The rebuilding of the French army began immediately after the suppression of the Commune. Despite recent defeats and the accusations of brutality made against it by the Left, the army found itself popular amongst the upper and middle classes, while the working classes accepted the obligations of the call-up every year. Uppermost in the minds of most people was the belief that, sooner rather than later, it would be necessary to fight Germany again, either to regain the provinces lost in 1871 or, as was actually to happen in 1914, to repel another invasion. Either of these contingencies was thought imminent throughout the age known as *La Belle Epoque*. So much was this the case that many of the younger and more ambitious officers would avoid colonial service for fear of missing the 'Big Show' in Europe, although it was the colonial troops, the long-service volunteers of the Foreign Legion, the Infanterie Coloniale and the native African troops who were almost continuously engaged on active service and thus had most opportunities for gaining distinction. When war came in 1914 it was under Joffre, an experienced colonial general, that the French army went to war, and many of his best subordinate commanders had had colonial experience. These appointments came as something of a surprise. Colonial officers, though hardy and brave, had not shown up well from the point of view of brains during the Franco-Prussian War. However, the colonial generals of 1914-18 proved much better material.

The scars left by the fall of the Empire, the loss of the war, and the events of the Commune began to heal during the first twenty years of the life of the Third Republic, but there were relapses which were serious enough, and which might have proved fatal, not only to the army but to France. That this was not the case was due, in large measure, to the fact that the army generally managed to keep aloof from politics and religious controversy. This was remarkable since there were, apart from the various civilian and financial scandals that disfigured the era, two sensational affairs involving the army.

Between 1887 and 1889 General Georges Boulanger, who was Minister of War for a short time, rose to a position of immense power. He had the support of Clemenceau and a considerable following at a time of general dissatisfaction and fierce anti-German feeling. In 1889 he appeared poised to lead a right-wing coup but, perhaps just in time, Clemenceau withdrew his support. It would seem that Boulanger made the mistake of relying on support from the crowd and his political followers rather than from his fellow soldiers. He lost his nerve and fled to Brussels, ending his life by shooting himself on his mistress's grave.

The amount of false witness, forgery and character assassination which was practised in the higher ranks of the army at the expense of the unfortunate and completely innocent Dreyfus, caused a great revulsion of feeling against the army when the truth finally became known. This revulsion destroyed not only the perpetrators of the affair but also affected very many officers who had had no connection with it. These suffered because there was a general reaction amongst politicians against the army. Catholics, Conservatives and anti-Dreyfusards were linked together, and a careful and suspicious watch was kept on officers deemed to go too often to church. For many radical politicians religion was akin to treason.

Below: Captain Dreyfus at the beginning of the affair which was to shake the very foundations of the Republic and its army, 1894.

Opposite: Foreign legionnaires in their canteen, c. 1900.

But while the Dreyfus case dragged on from 1894 to 1906 Europe moved from crisis to crisis and in the midst of the violent disputes the business of strengthening the army went on, despite the continued existence of an anti-militarist spirit amongst intellectuals and leaders of the Left.

During the last years of the century, the great advance technically had been in the sphere of artillery. Otherwise, prior to the development of the internal combustion engine, there was little new, and the question of effectives, that is, the number of men available, was of overwhelming importance. Between 1871 and 1893 the number of men of military age in France and Germany grew at about an equal rate, so that by the latter date the armies were of almost equal strength, with the French army totalling 453,000 and the German 457,000.

This state of affairs was reflected in the development of French planning for war. Plans made in 1875 under the shock of defeat were purely defensive; the principal aim in war would be to hold the lines of the Meurthe and Moselle and the fortifications at Toul, Verdun and Epinal.

In 1877 the Germans, in event of war, intended to give priority to the western front and attack France, while standing on the defensive against Russia. Two years later, however, they changed their minds and planned a regrouping of their forces, with fourteen corps on the eastern front and only four and a half on the west. The intention was to hold the French at bay, while Russia was attacked and defeated.

In the decade that followed, French self-confidence was reborn and flourished excessively. In 1889 it was decided that, when war came, the army was to go over to the offensive under the provisions of what was known as Plan 10, which called for attacks on Metz and Strasbourg. The length of national service was fixed at three years for all. Since the Franco-Prussian War, each annual class had been divided into two halves, one of which had to serve for five years, while the other, its members selected by lot, was released after twelve months service.

By 1893 the gap between the French and German birth rates was large, and the French sought and obtained an alliance with Russia. At this time the German plan was again changed and emerged from high-level discussions as the famous Schlieffen Plan in 1891, with seven-eighths of the German forces in the west and a small force screening East Prussia.

The period of military service in France was reduced to two years in 1905, but re-established at three years in 1913. This change gave France more men under arms in peace-time than Germany, although the proportion of the population of the two countries was seven to four in favour of Germany. In addition, in peace-time the French forces included 90,000 colonial troops from Africa whose picturesque uniforms used to steal the show at the great Parisian reviews on 14 July: the Spahis, cavalry in their long white cloaks; Turcos, Algerian riflemen; Zouaves, European infantry wearing native uniforms with red baggy trousers, red caps with black tassels and short blue jackets; and Senegalese sharpshooters. Then came long-service volunteers of the Foreign Legion from all over the world with their white cap covers and a slow solemn marching step adopted after years of experience marching across the deserts of North Africa. The Legion's great rivals were the Colonial Infantry, French Europeans who wore a small gold anchor as a cap badge as a reminder of the pre-1900 days when the French colonies were administered by the Ministry of Marine. All these could only be rivalled for glamour by the Cuirassiers and the Republican Guard with their gleaming breast plates and long horse-hair tails hanging from the crests of their brightly polished helmets. Somewhat surprisingly, breast plates and helmets, the latter with a cloth cover, were worn into battle during the first weeks of the campaign of 1914. The multi-coloured uniforms of the African troops were soon replaced by blue in the trenches. Three-quarters of a million Africans served in France as soldiers or as labourers in the rear.

While political disputes, technical progress and the moves of the great game of diplomacy were all going on, the more serious of French soldiers were thinking deeply and, as it turned out erroneously, on the conduct of the next war. The most important group came to the conclusion that what was required was a development of the offensive spirit. They believed that the lessons of history and the traditions of the French army called for a return to that spirit, which they recalled had given France victory in many battles. In addition, they believed that one of the lessons of 1870-1

Below: A typical foreign legionnaire in marching order.

Opposite: An Algerian rifleman in his light blue 'Zouave' type uniform, c. 1913.

had been that French troops lacked the ability to stand on the defensive under a prolonged storm of fire. The chief propagator of these views was a brilliant but misguided staff officer, Colonel de Grandmaison, and the fearful casualties of the battles of the frontiers in August 1914 were the result. The immediate French reaction on the appearance of the Germans was to attack, and these attacks were met by Germans with massed rifle and machine-gun fire, the effects of which had not been foreseen. They were summed up thus: 'In 1914 a Frenchman belonging to the army had two chances of life and one of being killed. He had hardly any chance of remaining without a wound', and long lines of blue and red clad figures lay in swathes over the green hills and fields of northern France.

FRANCE

History and traditions The nineteenth century was a period of recurrent crisis for the French army. It began with the fall of Napoleon I and two years of foreign occupation. It ended with the army trapped in the uncertainties of national politics and the menial task of maintaining civil order. The repercussions of the Dreyfus affair and the 'index card crisis' (arising from the Republican War Minister's practice of compiling files on the political opinions of army officers) caused a rift between the officer corps and the country it served, and during the period 1900-11 the number of candidates attending Saint-Cyr and Saint-Maixent fell by more than half. The armed forces had achieved victory in Belgium, Algeria, the Crimea, Italy, and the newly-won territories of the Empire, but defeat in the Franco-Prussian War of 1870-1 dominated military thinking in the decades before the First World War. That the army was able to regain its internal stability and present a united front with the nation in 1914 was due almost entirely to one external factor, the militarism of Germany. Faced with German encroachments in colonial areas under France's influence, notably at Tangier and Agadir in Morocco, France became convinced that war with Germany was inevitable.

Strength The peace establishment of the French army in 1900 totalled 27,450 officers and 517,000 men. The war establishment, which included the reserve of the active army, the territorial army and its reserve, could call upon approximately 4,660,000 men of all ranks, of whom about 500,000 were untrained.

System of recruiting France was divided into eighteen military districts with a nineteenth in Algeria. Each district was allocated an army corps which maintained a recruiting depot and mobilization cadres. The yearly intake of recruits from the districts amounted to 230,000 men and an additional 21,000 volunteers.

Terms of service Service in the army was obligatory between the ages of twenty and forty-five with a normal requirement of three years in the active army, ten years in its reserve, and six years each in the territorial army and reserve.

Organization In peace and war the military organization of France was based upon the army corps of two divisions of infantry and one brigade of cavalry with supporting troops and artillery. In 1900 there were nineteen army corps, but by 1914 the number had been increased to twenty-four.

Infantry The infantry was organized as 145 sub-divisional and eighteen regional regiments with thirty battalions of Chasseurs à Pied and four regiments of light infantry. Each of the sub-divisional regiments had four battalions. Much of the infantry was drawn from the colonies, and by 1914 they represented 9% of the army's effective strength; the most renowned were the regiments of Zouaves recruited from the white population of North Africa. The Foreign Legion drew its men not from the indigenous population of the Empire but from European volunteers who sought escape and adventure in war.

Above: French infantry in their linen fatigue uniforms, Eure et Loire, August 1912.
Right: French artillery with their famous 75 field gun on manoeuvres, 1913.

Cavalry In 1900 there were eighty-nine regiments of cavalry established as thirteen Cuirassiers, thirty-one Dragoons, twenty-one Chasseurs, fourteen Hussars, six Chasseurs d'Afrique, and four Spahis. A regiment consisted of four active, and one depot squadron and during war each squadron numbered five officers and 155 other ranks. The Spahis were light cavalry recruited from the native population of Algeria and these born horsemen, attired in their native dress, presented a colourful but anachronistic spectacle in war.

Artillery The artillery comprised forty regiments of field and horse artillery forming nineteen brigades of two regiments with two regiments remaining. There were also eighteen fortress artillery battalions. Each brigade was attached to an army corps with one regiment assigned to the divisional artillery and one to the corps artillery.

Reserves France maintained three lines of reserves; that of the active army, the territorial army, and the reserve of the territorial army. For mobilization, training, and administration the units of the reserve and the territorial army were attached to the corresponding units of the active army. The war strength of the reserve of the active army was approximately 1,300,000 men.

Territorial army The principal units of the territorial army were 145 infantry regiments, seven battalions of Chasseurs à Pied, ten battalions of Zouaves, 150 squadrons of cavalry, nineteen regiments of artillery, and eighteen battalions of engineers. In combination with its reserve, the territorial army had a total strength of 2,270,000 officers and men, and in war they were employed primarily in the defence of fortresses and lines of communication.

France's military organization was designed above all else to compensate for the nation's population problem. This was not, as in the case of Austria, a question of minorities which might weaken the army's unity and effectiveness, for among the leading military powers France had probably the most homogeneous population; it was simply that as a nation she could produce but 60% of the potential manpower of Germany. The balance could be redressed to a certain extent by calling upon her colonies, but this dependence raised political as well as military difficulties. Colonial troops were to prove of value in European warfare particularly in the attack, and during good weather. Their effectiveness fell sharply, however, under constant fire in defensive positions and during inclement weather. The military programme of France sprang, therefore, not from a deep appreciation of the nature of modern war but from the apparently inescapable logic of her declining birth rate.

A French hussar greeting one of the first British troops to land in France with the British expeditionary force in 1914. The sky blue and red uniform of the French soldier has changed little from that worn

*During manoeuvres in the west of France in 1913,
airships were used for aerial reconnaissance.*

*The French Minister of War inspects troops dressed in the new prototype
uniform, which was so disliked that it was never introduced, Paris 1910.*

3 AUSTRIA-HUNGARY

In July 1914 the Austro-Hungarian armies marched to war for the last time, after nearly four centuries of fighting, during which they had taken part in more than 7000 actions great and small.

From the Thirty Years War to the French Revolution, Austrian troops were considered to be the best and most experienced soldiers in the world. They had been almost continuously engaged for years in border affrays with the Turks on their eastern and southern frontiers, and in Europe, wars against France and Prussia had made them thoroughly skilled in waging war according to the manner of the eighteenth century. However, neither they nor any other European army at that time were ready to meet the combination of leadership, numbers and morale which gave almost invincible strength to the armies of the French Revolution and Empire. Five times during the Napoleonic Wars, Austria was among the European powers which formed coalitions against France, and three times Austria was defeated in the field. Within a few years she again took up arms and, in the end, Austrian troops were amongst the allied armies of occupation in France.

After the fall of Napoleon I, occupation duties were the principal task of the Austrian army, for it became clear that the Austrian-held provinces of northern Italy were, and would continue to be, in a permanent state of unrest. This need to hold them in check meant that the Austrian army had to be maintained in a constant state of alert and thus it never had an opportunity during these years to sink

into the monotonous regime of the peace-time armies of the 1820s and the 1830s. During the years 1848 and 1849 the Austrians had won vital battles against Sardinian or Piedmontese troops as well as those of other Italian states, which had risen in rebellion against the overlordship of Vienna. However, there were not enough Austrian soldiers to suppress the Hungarian rising of 1848 as well. This was the most severe test to which the Austro-Hungarian monarchy had been subjected and it shows clearly the strains on its armies — recruited from the various races and religions which composed the Austrian Empire and the Kingdom of Hungary.

Trouble had begun in 1846 with a rising by the Poles of Galicia against the German-Austrian government of Vienna. This was put down with the help of the Ruthenians, who had long complained of the treatment they had received from the Poles. This has been described as an example of the policy of 'divide and rule', but it was not deliberate. Instead it was part of a general situation in which each of the races of the Empire had bitter enemies amongst their neighbours and fellow subjects.

On 17 May 1848 rioting of Left against Right in Vienna sent the Emperor Ferdinand I to Innsbruck ('for the benefit of his health' according to the official communiqué). In Bohemia, Czechs rose against the German-Austrian administration. In Croatia the Croats rebelled against their Hungarian rulers and, at the same time, Jellachich, the Croatian leader, urged Croatian troops in Italy to fight the Italians and remain loyal to Vienna. The Hungarians declared themselves independent. Austria appealed to Russia for help and after campaigns lasting eleven months, Hungary was overrun by the Russians, aided by the Croats and stiffened by German-Austrian officers.

Eventually the tumult of 1848-9 died down. The long-service, professional army had been loyal throughout, thanks in part to a certain amount of discretion in drafting units; Italian troops, for example, were not sent to fight in Italy. The epileptic and feeble-minded Emperor Ferdinand abdicated in favour of his eighteen-year-old nephew, Francis Joseph, who lived to within two years of the end of the Hapsburg Empire.

Various ancient feudal obligations had been abrogated as an outcome of the disturbances and for a few years it seemed as though the damage had been repaired; but that was not the case. There had been a divorce between Austria and Hungary, two halves of the dual monarchy, although they were both still under the same sovereign. This was a state of affairs which was to ruin both halves and Europe as well.

The Austrian government made elaborate declarations of gratitude to the Tsar for his help in putting down the Hungarian rebellion, but an observer at the time remarked 'Austria will astonish the world by her ingratitude' and this, in fact, is what happened, for when the Crimean War broke out Vienna remained deaf to suggestions from St Petersburg that the debt of gratitude

Opposite: Austrian field smithy at Veile in 1864.

51

should be repaid by intervention on Russia's side, and Austria's final refusal to cooperate convinced Russia that it was necessary to make peace.

In 1858 Napoleon III decided it was time that the military glories of France and of the name of Napoleon should be further refurbished after the Crimean War. Cavour, the Sardinian Prime Minister, was, moreover, persuading him that the unity of Italy was a cause he should espouse, not only for the practical reason that a united Italy would be an ally of France but also because, looking back over his shoulder, he could catch a glimpse of the young Italian patriot he had himself been in his youth. He was reminded of this by the Italian patriots (of the more extreme sort), who endeavoured to blow him up, together with his Empress on their way to the opera in Paris on 14 January 1858.

After that incident the fear remained with Napoleon that the attempt might be repeated and, partly to appease his possible assassins, he decided on the war in alliance with Sardinia against Austria, in which he displayed that fatal mixture of dash and irresolution which was so characteristic of him. Having launched his war, he became worried about the consequences, though to be fair to him, it is also probable that he was truly shocked as he rode over the battlefields of Solferino and Magenta and saw the horrors which he had instigated.

In 1866 Austria was again defeated in the Seven Weeks War under circumstances which go far to illustrate the mentality of the Austrian Emperor. The most able general in his army was Ludwig, Ritter von Benedek, who for years had specialized in plans and preparations for a campaign on the Austrian southern front in defence of Venice and the surrounding province of Venetia. At the

Men of the Imperial Austrian Infantry Regiment No. 25 flanked by Royal Hungarian infantry on the left, and by Austro-Hungarian sailors on the right, c. 1885.

same time preparations on the northern front were being made by the Archduke Albert. It was rightly judged by Vienna that the Archduke's prospects of success were slimmer than those of Benedek and it was further appreciated that, were he to be defeated, it would be a very serious blow to the prestige of the Imperial house. Accordingly, the two generals were hastily switched round, the Archduke won his easy victory over the Italians at Custozza, while Benedek lost at Sadowa, and received all the blame and odium, without protest. This treatment of a skilful and honest soldier, shabby to the point of sleaziness, was far too typical of the conduct of the Hapsburg court.

After Sadowa it was essential that the Austrians should strengthen their position and to do this they were obliged to swallow their pride and obtain a rapprochement with Hungary on Hungary's terms. The aristocratic ruling caste of Hungary hailed the conclusion of this agreement as a great triumph for liberty. It was, indeed, a triumph for them, though not for the people of their Hungarian domains, for in all only 6% of the population received the vote, and the fact that 50% of the people at the beginning of this century could not read and write was to have its effect on the quality of the Hungarian army.

By this time there were nine different languages spoken as native tongues in Austrian or Hungarian units: German, Hungarian, Italian, Romanian, Czech or Slovak, Serbo-Croat, Slovene, Polish, and Ruthenian. To deal with this situation, as far as it could be dealt with, eighty words of command were established, all in German, and all other communications to the units were made in their own languages. In addition there had developed a kind of unofficial dialect known as 'Army Slav'.

Only 28% of the strength of the Austro-Hungarian army were German Austrians, 44% were Slavs and 18% Hungarians, with the Romanian and Italian peoples of the Empire contributing 8% and 2%. There were pronounced differences between the mental levels of the different races within the dual monarchy and a higher proportion of the more intelligent Hungarian, Czech and German peoples were to be found in the cavalry, the artillery and the technical branches of the army than in the infantry, 67% of whose total strength was made up of Slavs. Throughout this period it was the custom to base units in areas where the populace were of a different nation for the sake of internal stability.

In 1878 the Austrian army began its last successful campaign. The powers whose intervention or whose self-control at the Congress of Berlin had contributed to the preservation of Turkey in Europe, though not of its territorial integrity, all claimed their rewards from the Turks. Russia's satellites, Romania, Bulgaria, Serbia and Montenegro all received territorial gains. Britain, having promised to uphold the cause of Turkey, received Cyprus as a base to help her to do so, while Austria received permission to occupy the Serbo-Croatian provinces of Bosnia and Herzegovina and the Sanjak of Novi Bazar. In these territories the Austrian army

Umpires, with white bands on their kepis, at Royal Hungarian army manoeuvres near Güns in 1893.

was in action for the last time before 1914. The operation was, essentially, the occupation of an extremely hilly region whose inhabitants had been waging intermittent war against the Turks for some four hundred years. They now shifted their target from the old to the new occupant and, within forty years, had helped destroy his throne and shot dead his heir. Although an easy task had been expected in Vienna, it still required nearly 300,000 men and three months before Bosnia was pacified.

In the years after the Bosnian campaign the Austrian army sank deeper and deeper into a peaceful routine which progressively robbed it of its capability for war. This process became clearly noticeable to Austria's German ally, and in 1904 General Hülsen Häseler, Chief of the Military Cabinet of Kaiser William II, was sent to Vienna to try to secure the adoption of a programme of reforms which would make the Austrian army fit for service in a twentieth-century European war. He was rebuffed by the Chief of the Austrian General Staff, Baron von Beck, who had held his post for twenty-four years. Francis Joseph wanted, above all, a quiet life and an army which merely looked well on parade.

In 1906 Francis Joseph fell ill, and Francis Ferdinand, his nephew and heir, replaced him at the annual manoeuvres of the combined services in Dalmatia. The General and the heir to the throne clashed fatally and immediately, not on the level of higher strategic planning but on that of mitigating the rigours of life on manoeuvres. Beck convoked the Archduke to witness the beginning of an exercise at five o'clock in the morning; nothing happened until seven. The Archduke showed his displeasure and soon had his revenge. Beck enjoyed his food very much and liked to take his time. Francis Ferdinand decided to talk to Beck's staff at the end of dinner, cutting short the General's time at table. However, when the meeting began the General arrived late, holding in his two hands the uneaten remainder of his dinner, two rich cream cakes, which he proceeded to eat as he listened to His Imperial and Royal Highness.

The too-early morning rendezvous, the cream cakes, and the fact that Beck was clearly incapable of performing his duties led to his replacement by a man of a very different kind. In the pacifist reaction immediately following the First World War, it was one of the stereotypes that generals on both sides were bloodthirsty men, longing to win 'glittering prizes' with their swords. When archives were opened and history properly studied it was discovered that of the hundreds of generals ranged against each other the only one who openly urged war was Franz Conrad von Hötzendorf who in 1906, at the age of fifty-four, was appointed Chief of the Austro-Hungarian General Staff. For the previous seven years the conviction had grown within him that Austria could not survive without a successful war against either or both Italy and Serbia to bring to an end the propaganda campaigns which they were waging amongst the Italian and Yugoslav minorities within the Austrian borders.

While beginning a widespread campaign of reform within the army he continued to labour this point with Francis Ferdinand. In 1909 he wished for war with Serbia and in 1911 he resigned after he had failed to obtain permission to attack Italy. He was reappointed in 1912 and again tried to start a war with Serbia or, if necessary, with Russia. Finally, in July 1914, Francis Ferdinand died and he at last got his way. His conduct of Austria's war against Russia and Italy is reckoned by many good judges as having been of as high a standard as any shown in the First World War but his troops were not always equal to the demands he made of them.

Right up to the end of the First World War the Hungarians continued to demand their own army. In the general process of appeasing them after 1866 they were allowed a second line force, the Honved, which had to be paralleled by a similar Austrian force, the Landwehr. These two forces came under the Austrian and Hungarian governments respectively, while the first line troops were under the combined Austro-Hungarian Ministry of War. The Austro-Hungarian Empire only shared three ministries which operated for both nations, the ministries of War, Foreign Affairs and Finance. Combined Austrian and Hungarian ground troops were referred to as 'K und K' — Kaiserlich und Königlich (Imperial and Royal), Austrian units were referred to as 'K K' — Kaiserlich –Königlich (Imperial –Royal), for the Emperor of Austria was also King of Bohemia, and 'K' — Kiralyi –Royal (Hungarian). On the eve of the First World War, the combined peace-time strength of all three totalled about 350,000. Mobilization brought about a three-fold increase in the strength, giving a total of forty-nine infantry divisions. The total number of men with the colours at this time was 3,350,000 but of these rather less than half, 1,421,000, were front line troops on active service. Altogether during the First World War 8,000,000 men served in the three services, of whom more than 1,000,000 were killed and 1,691,000 taken prisoner.

Right: An Austrian infantryman proudly poses in his walking-out uniform (he would never have been allowed to wear little trinkets or his watch chain when on duty), Vienna, c. 1900.

Below: Scene in the barracks of Pioneer Section 33 of the Royal and Imperial army, c. 1900.

AUSTRIA-HUNGARY

History and traditions Despite the shattering defeats of Ulm and Austerlitz in 1805 the Austrian army emerged from the Napoleonic Wars, and from its part in the occupation of France, with renewed prestige and self-confidence. The repossession of the Napoleonic kingdom of Italy together with the war indemnities paid by France allowed Austria to maintain large forces drawn from all quarters of the dual monarchy. For a time, indeed, the army remained one of the most important links between the constituent nations, but with defeat, first at the hands of France (1859) and then of Prussia (1866), and with the growth of nationalism the heterogeneous nature of the Empire came to pose acute problems for the armed forces. Foremost was the question of language since recruits were drawn from nine linguistic nationalities each of which had a variety of dialects. The use of German as the language of command failed to provide a solution, since although 75% of the officers were of Germanic origin only 25% of the enlisted men were fluent in the language. The impact of nationalism was particularly apparent during war when the influence of reservists, who were openly receptive to pan-Slavic and Russian propaganda, was brought to bear on serving troops. By 1914 only Hungarian, German and Bosnian regiments could be deployed safely on any front, whoever the foe.

Strength During peace the dual monarchy could dispose of an army of some 350,000 officers and men, but in time of war this strength could be expanded to approximately 3,000,000.

Recruiting system For the purposes of recruiting Austria-Hungary was divided into fifteen army-corps districts and the district of Zara. Each army corps raised men from its own district with the exception of the 15th Corps, based upon Bosnia and Herzegovina, which recruited only infantry locally and relied for the remainder of its troops upon other areas. Recruits were selected by lot for service in the active army, the reserve, or the Landwehr.

Terms of service Army service was compulsory for every healthy male from the age of nineteen to forty-two although enrolment was not usually invoked until the age of twenty-one. Using a system of drawing lots, the lowest numbers were required to serve for three years in the line, seven in the reserve and two in the Landwehr. The middle numbers were allotted two years in the Landwehr, while the highest numbers received exemption in peace-time. The ranks of the Landsturm were filled with those men who had completed twelve years of service and who remained fit for duty.

Officers In contrast to the service required of men in the rank of private and the four grades of under-officer (corporal, sergeant, sergeant-major, cadet), the commissioned officer was liable for service to the age of sixty. The majority of commissions were taken by the cadets who had spent three years, between the ages of fourteen and seventeen, at one of the fifteen cadet schools. In addition there were two higher academies, the Wiener-Neustadt producing officers for the infantry and cavalry, and the Technical Academy of Vienna training officers for the artillery and engineers. Once commissioned, an officer received promotion partly by selection and partly by seniority, and a candidate who passed through the ranks of NCOs could only be promoted to cadet by examination. Although the officer corps reflected the aristocratic hierarchy to be found throughout the Empire, it was far less exclusive than that of the British and German armies and off-duty comradeship in particular transcended the distinctions of class and position.

Organization As a result of Austria's defeat in 1866 the army was largely reorganized on the model of the Prussian military system. The active army comprised the Imperial and Royal troops while the reserve was formed by the Austrian and Hungarian Landwehr and Landsturm. The war organization was based on fifteen army corps made up of thirty-one infantry and five cavalry divisions and 224 field batteries. To augment these corps there were an additional fourteen divisions of Landwehr infantry and three divisions of army and Landwehr cavalry.

Infantry The infantry of the active army was divided into line regiments and Jäger, or rifle, battalions. Each of the 102 line regiments mobilized a regimental staff; four battalions of four field companies, and a depot battalion of four companies. The Jägers comprised an Imperial Regiment and thirty battalions.

Cavalry The regular cavalry was organized in forty-two regiments of which fifteen were dragoons, sixteen hussars, and eleven Uhlans.

Artillery The artillery was divided into field and fortress regiments, the former consisting of fourteen corps artillery regiments and forty-two independent battery divisions, and the latter of six regiments and three battalions. Every field regiment had two battery divisions of four batteries each and every independent division had three batteries. The divisions numbered one to twenty-eight were attached to the infantry divisions of the first fourteen army corps while the remainder served with the Landwehr infantry.

Engineers The technical branches of the army comprised engineers, pioneers and railway and telegraph troops organized into two battalion regiments, each in war consisting of about 330 officers and 12,700 men.

Landwehr The Landwehr was divided into two distinct sections, that of Austria (the 'KK' Landwehr) and that of Hungary (the 'K' Landwehr or Honved). During peace the Landwehr battalions were maintained as cadres but on mobilization they were rapidly expanded and the Hungarian battalions were generally larger than those of the Austrian Landwehr.

Landsturm The Landsturm was again divided into Austrian and Hungarian sections and its total strength was in excess of 900,000 men, although only some 25% could be considered as adequately trained.

Although a potent force on paper, the efficiency of the Austro-Hungarian army was undermined by the racial mixture of the recruits it drew from the dual monarchy. The process of disintegration was slow but sure and from the opening campaign of 1914 there was a growing number of desertions by non-Austrian troops, sometimes spectacularly engulfing a whole regiment in a matter of hours. Thus although based on the German model the Austro-Hungarian army was in nearly every respect inferior to it.

Members of the Royal Hungarian Honved Hussar Regiment No. 1 in field service order, c. 1911. The hussar on the right is an officer's orderly.

*Above: Officers of a Moslem
Bosnia-Herzegovinian
infantry regiment in 1914.*

*Right: Church parade during
the Austrian advance into
Galicia, autumn 1914.*

4 RUSSIA

Far left: General of Engineers, E. I. Todleben, who constructed the fortifications at Sevastopol.

Left: Typical Russian soldiers of the Crimean War.

Below: A battery in the Kornilov Bastion (Malakoff Hill) during the siege of Sevastopol.

During 1972 the official Soviet naval review *Morskoi Sbornik* published a series of articles by the Admiral of the Fleet of the Soviet Union S. G. Gorshkov, Chief of the Soviet Naval Staff, on naval history and, especially, Russian naval history. In the course of one article he stated that the total number of Russian casualties during the Crimean War had been 750,000. Previously this figure had been estimated in the West to be about 250,000. There were thus half a million more men lost than had hitherto been accounted for, and as the number of Russians killed and wounded in action, together with prisoners, was fairly certainly established, it was clear that the other half million had been lost outside the war zone. The most likely explanation is that the men died of cold and hunger making their way on foot across Russia in midwinter at a time when there were very few railways, roads or organized supply depots.

In the Hermitage Museum in Leningrad there hung, and probably still hangs, a battle picture from the Russo-Turkish War of 1828-9, depicting an incident in which a Russian infantry regiment filled in a ditch with its own living bodies so that the artillery could get forward. The gruesome horror of the picture is no doubt exaggerated but it does represent what was expected of Russian soldiers.

The quality of the Russian troops was not of paramount importance and even at the outbreak of the First World War probably half of the men in the ranks could neither read nor write. Nevertheless, despite the manifold imperfections that were obvious at the time, the fact remained that towards the end of the nineteenth century, the Russian army, with a million men under arms in peace-time and the ability to mobilize 114 infantry divisions in war, was the largest in the world; it hung over Europe and Asia as a huge threat to its enemies and its alliance was clearly a prize of enormous value.

After the Crimea the Russian army was occupied in pushing the boundaries of the empire eastward to the Pacific and southward to the Pamirs and operating against the Polish rebels in 1863. In 1876 the condition of Turkey, the country referred to by Tsar Nicholas I as 'the sick man of Europe', took another turn for the worse. The country's economy was in complete chaos and bankruptcy seemed to be staved off only by a series of expedients none of which seemed possible to repeat. The subject races of the Balkan peninsula, feeling the central authority of Constantinople growing weaker almost month by month, began to shove and strain at the ramshackle structure of the Turkish Empire. In 1876 it was the turn of the tiny semi-independent principality of Serbia to shove and a brief war was started. Russia, who had been bent for over 150 years on the piecemeal diminution if not destruction of Turkish power, was watchful and contributed to the Serbian cause by lending to the Serbian insurgent army a commander-in-chief, General Tchernaiev. Neither for the first nor the last time did the Turks surprise the world by their power of military recovery in a crisis, and now they easily defeated the Serbs under their Russian general. Using

Turkish atrocities against the Orthodox Bulgars (the so-called Bulgarian Atrocities) as a pretext, the Russians and their Romanian allies declared war on Turkey and began two invasions of the country, one over the Danube through Bulgaria and the other across the Caucasus into Armenia. The campaign in the Caucasus ended with the capture by the Russians of the important fortresses of Ardahan and Kars which they retained at the peace conference that took place at Berlin in the following year. However, it was in Bulgaria that the fiercest and most famous fighting took place, around the town of Plevna. A combined Russian and Romanian force under Grand Duke Nicholas, brother of Tsar Alexander II, crossed the Danube and marched against Adrianople, with, as its goal, Constantinople. To check the Russians the Turks, under Osman Pasha, took up a position on their flank at Plevna and dug in; if the Russians were to be able to continue their advance the Turkish threat from Plevna had to be removed. Accordingly the town was first assailed and then besieged. The fight for Plevna was a classic battle, a milestone in the development of warfare on land. The Turks had no fortifications in the traditional sense but surrounded the town with a series of shallow trenches, mostly mere ditches, but defended with great spirit by the 40,000-strong garrison which had the advantage of being equipped with the new American Peabody-Martini magazine rifles, very much superior to the Russian weapons. When Plevna fell after a resistance of nearly five months, the Russians advanced almost to Constantinople and an armistice was arranged.

Two of the Russian leaders in this fighting were very notable soldiers indeed. It had soon become clear that Plevna could not be taken by storm but would have to be subjected to a lengthy siege; for this it was necessary to construct elaborate field works. The Chief Engineer appointed for this was General Todleben who over twenty years previously, although at the time only a captain, had been in charge of the fortifications at Sevastopol. In the forefront of the Russian attacks at Plevna was Mikhail Skobelev, who had been promoted general four years previously at the age of thirty-two. He was both brave and flamboyant, leading his attacking columns of infantry riding a white horse and wearing a white sheepskin cap. In his brilliant white uniform, he was an ideal target for Turkish marksmen, but was never once hit. After the war he became involved in politics and made a number of untimely speeches prophesying war between Russia and Germany, for which he was rebuked. He died suddenly, following a heart attack in Moscow, at the age of fifty-nine.

The appointment of both Todleben and Skobelev to important commands at Sevastopol and Plevna was characteristic of the Russian Tsarist army in the last decades of its existence. Serious efforts were made to see that suitable officers were promoted to general rank by the age of forty. This turned out to be a very hit-and-miss procedure; some brilliant officers of middle rank receiving accelerated promotion as well as some thoroughly

Above: A Russian camp in Turkey, Russo-Turkish War, 1877-8.

Tsar Alexander II in guard hussar uniform, c. 1870.

Below: Grand Duke Nicolai-Nicolaievitch, Commander-in-Chief of the Russian army during the Russo-Turkish War, with his escort, 1878.

*Russian guardsmen with their regimental colour, on one side of which appeared a religious ikon,
and on the other the cypher of the reigning Tsar. The uniform is the simplified green (actually almost black)*

Above and below: Guard artillery at gun drill, c. 1890. Right: Types of Life Guard Cossacks in 1900.

worthless ones. Conservatives in foreign armies criticized the Russian procedure on the ground that promotion was so rapid that most of the young generals' time was spent on staff appointments with the result that they had very little time in command of troops.

An officer whose career corresponded closely to this pattern and who was to achieve quick promotion and high command at an early age and was finally to bear, unjustly, the blame for a great Russian defeat was Alexei Nikolaievitch Kuropatkin. Born in 1848, he was Chief of Staff to Skobelev at Plevna, wrote the standard and authoritative history of the campaign and, four years after the war, was promoted major general at the age of thirty-four, having in the meantime distinguished himself in the campaigns then in progress in Central Asia. His most sensational exploit was the conduct of a 500-mile march from Tashkent to Geok Tepe which ended in the storming of the latter. He was a good staff officer and a humane man but he lacked the capacity to take risks. As the crisis with Japan approached war he was appointed to command the Russian army in Manchuria, having been Minister of War in St Petersburg.

Left: General Kuropatkin, Commander-in-Chief of the Russian army in the Russo-Japanese War.

Below left: Russian artillery at rest during the advance into Manchuria in 1904.

Below right: Russian infantry march into Manchuria, 1904.

It was in Manchuria, a province of China, that all the land fighting of the war took place, although China was neutral throughout. The explanation of this state of affairs lay in the economic penetration of China then being practised on a large scale by the great powers and which had passed, as far as the Russians were concerned, from commercial exploitation to military occupation. The army was there on the pretext that it was necessary to protect the Russian-built and owned Chinese Eastern Railway, which ran across Manchuria from Chita in Siberia to Vladivostock, and the South Manchurian Railway which ran south from Mukden and Harbin to Port Arthur, the Russian naval base and ice-free port. This port had originally been Chinese but had been taken by the Japanese in their war with China in 1894. Russia, France and Germany then presented an ultimatum to Japan demanding its return to China. The Japanese complied, the Russians took over the port from the Chinese, made it the base of their Pacific Fleet and continued expansion into China and Korea. A long series of negotiations between Tokyo and St Petersburg followed, in the

middle of which the Japanese lost patience and, without warning, attacked the Russian fleet at Port Arthur on the night of 8-9 February 1904 just as nearly forty years later they attacked the United States fleet at Pearl Harbor.

In Britain and, to a large extent, in the United States, there was a great deal of sympathy and admiration for the Japanese, seen as a David challenging a Goliath, and a first glance at the available figures supports this view. Russia had a peace-time army of one million men serving five years which, it was claimed, could be increased to 4,500,000 on mobilization. On the other hand, the Japanese peace-time army was only 283,000, raised by maximum effort to 800,000 on mobilization. But while the whole first-line Japanese army could rapidly be deployed in the Manchurian war zone, there were only 83,000 Russian troops in the entire area east of Lake Baikal, together with some 55,000 fortress troops and those protecting the railway.

Camp scene during the Russo-Japanese War.

For reinforcements and supplies the Russians depended on the famous Trans-Siberian Railway which had just been completed, except for a hundred-mile gap around the southern shore of Lake Baikal where men and freight had to be unloaded and marched by road, or in winter over the ice. The construction of the railway had been a very great engineering feat, but to save time and money it had been built with only a single track, and the rails and rolling stock were light and quite unsuitable for the heavy traffic which conditions of war demanded of them.

The Japanese destroyer attack on Port Arthur had put the Russian fleet temporarily out of action, and, taking advantage of this, the Japanese began to land their army in Korea which, at this time, was also neutral. Their first objective was to cut off Port Arthur at the tip of the Liao-Tung peninsula. Commanded by General Kuroki, 40,000 Japanese troops landed at Chemulpo (Jinsen, near where the Americans landed in September 1950), then turned northward and lined up preparatory to crossing the Yalu.

On the other side of the river were 7000 Russians under General Zasulich, with orders from Kuropatkin to watch the enemy but not to become involved in a battle. However Zasulich, with a mixture of courage, insubordination and folly, decided on a stand on the Yalu. Afterwards he explained that, having recently been created a Knight of St George by the Tsar, he could not run away. Accordingly he fought, was beaten and forced to retreat. It was not a great battle but its outcome has been held, especially in the Far East, to have turned the world upside down. An Eastern power, until then deemed of the second rank, had defeated one of the great European powers. The Japanese next landed just outside Port Arthur, crossed the Liao-Tung peninsula and thus cut off the fortress from Kuropatkin, who had concentrated the main body of his forces some 150 miles away at Liao Yang on the South Manchurian Railway. There he planned to await reinforcements by land and by sea. The rate of arrival of the land force may be seen from the fact that it took a single regiment a month to travel from Russia to the front, via the

General Kuropatkin receives reports from his commanders in Manchuria, July 1904. The officers already wear khaki-coloured shirts, which were not to become standard until 1907.

Trans-Siberian Railway.

As for the Japanese, their Commander-in-Chief Marshal Oyama left the siege of Port Arthur to General Nogi's Third Army, while, with three other armies, he advanced on Kuropatkin at Liao Yang. Nogi was unable to wait to starve out Port Arthur because, far away in the Baltic, the Second Pacific Squadron was being organized. This was to sail around the world to reinforce the First Pacific Squadron, still a powerful force despite the losses which it had suffered during the first days of the war. If the two Russian squadrons linked up they would have at least a two to one superiority over the Japanese fleet and would be able to cut the communications between the Japanese army in Manchuria and its bases and sources of supply in Japan. Then the Russian army would be able to use the maps of Japan with which it had been liberally supplied for invasion purposes.

Meanwhile the Japanese, under Oyama, made their way northward and, on 25 August, challenged Kuropatkin at Liao Yang in the biggest battle of the war up to that time. Both sides were more or less equal in strength, with 100,000 men apiece. After eight days of heavy fighting the Russians broke off the battle and fell back on Mukden, the Manchurian capital, although their losses (16,500) were less than those of the Japanese (23,500). After this battle Kuropatkin's strategy remained the same, to wait for the arrival of the Second Squadron which, it was believed, would give Russia command of the sea.

Meanwhile Nogi's besieging army hurled themselves time and time again into the assault of Port Arthur. Modern warfare had never seen such fighting and European observers wondered if their troops could ever equal the tenacity and courage shown by both sides.

On 5 December the Japanese finally took 203 Metre Hill, from where they were able to open direct fire on the Russian warships in the harbour. This was the end of the First Pacific Squadron and Port Arthur itself surrendered on 1 January 1905. General Stoessel, the

Russian artillery in Peking during the Boxer Rebellion in 1900.

commander of the garrison, who is generally considered to have behaved with inefficiency and sheer stupidity, had been relieved of this post some months previously, but suppressed the relevant signal and remained, to the ruin of his command. After his return to Russia he was courtmartialled and sentenced to death but then reprieved. In the siege more than 30,000 Russians had been killed or wounded, and 25,000 more taken prisoner, while the Japanese had had 90,000 killed, wounded and sick.

By this time the Second Squadron, under Rozhestvensky, had only got as far as Madagascar, but nevertheless, despite the disaster of Port Arthur, it continued very slowly on its way.

The troops which had taken Port Arthur were now turned and sent north to face Kuropatkin in front of Mukden, where Oyama prepared to make another attack, to take place before the spring thaw because during the cold weather the frozen rivers were no obstacle to manoeuvres. In addition the outbreak of riots and the first signs of revolution in Russia were hindering the despatch of reinforcements to the army in Siberia.

Although the two armies were about equal in size the Japanese, by reason of their mobility (they sometimes covered fifty miles a day on foot) were able to turn both Russian flanks and on 10 March Kuropatkin ordered Mukden to be abandoned and the army to fall back on Tie Ling, some forty miles to the north.

This was the end of serious fighting on land. The Japanese began to plan attacks on Vladivostock and Harbin, but both sides were exhausted in different ways. Japan was very nearly bankrupt, to such an extent that, having ordered two new battleships, which were to be the largest in the world, it was discovered that there was not enough money to pay for the planned armament and inferior weapons had to be used. In Russia conditions were even more serious, since there the 1905 Revolution was beginning.

Despite the fall of Port Arthur, Rozhestvensky with his fleet continued on his way and, in one of the most complete victories in naval history, the whole force was either sunk or captured by the Japanese, save for a few minor vessels, in the Straits of Tsushima on 27-28 May 1905.

Kuropatkin, who after Mukden had been relieved of the supreme command in the Far East, wrote: 'Far from assisting our army Rozhestvensky brought it irreparable harm. It was the defeat of his

squadron at Tsushima that brought about negotiations and peace at a time when our army was ready to advance — a million strong.' Few agreed with him then, however, and no one at all does so now.

In the peace treaty concluded at Portsmouth, New Hampshire, under the aegis of President Theodore Roosevelt, the Japanese obtained the influence in Korea which enabled them to annex the whole Korean Empire in 1910. They received the southern half of the island of Sakhalin, but not the whole island for which they had asked, while the Russians were able to avoid payment of reparations. At the same time the Russians maintained their unofficial but nevertheless very real hold on north and central Manchuria.

Some lessons had been learned, however, from the war in Manchuria. Twenty years after Tannenberg, I toured the battlefield with the German official historian of the action. Shallow trenches everywhere indicated where the Russian positions had been. The Germans had, throughout the early days of the war on the Eastern Front, been surprised to see how the Russians, even if halted for only half an hour, immediately started to dig themselves in, a practice which captured Russian officers attributed to their experience in their war with Japan.

The Russian troops returned home from Manchuria to find discontent in factories and on the farms, with mutinies in the navy. Although the army had its share of grievances, increased by the slowness of demobilization when the troubles broke out late in 1905, it appears to have obeyed orders and not sided with the crowds in the way which made possible the success of the February Revolution in 1917.

After the Russo-Japanese war the danger of war in Europe grew every year as the Germans and Austrians sought to take advantage of Russia's weakness. A strengthening of the Russian army and rebuilding of the shattered navy were urgently necessary. The money was forthcoming from international loans, mostly from France, for as long as Russia was weak the menace to France from Germany remained.

Although from 1909 work on the re-armament of Russia went ahead there was not time to fill the great gaps, nor was there the required technical ability or administrative efficiency to do the work. Old habits persisted, symbolized by the way in which the Russian troops in their characteristic long greatcoats still marched and drilled with their bayonets always fixed because Suvarov had distrusted the muskets of his day (1729-1800) and preferred to rely on the bayonet.

In August 1914 Russia went to war under-armed and under-equipped. By the beginning of December of that year only 300,000 rounds of ammunition remained for the artillery (a week's supply if a big battle was in progress) and a million rifles had been lost out of a total stock at the beginning of hostilities of 5,500,000. Casualties since the beginning of August had amounted to 1,350,000. To replace these, there were 800,000 men, well-equipped, except for the fact that there were no weapons for them.

RUSSIA

History and traditions At the end of the twenty-two-year struggle with Sweden in 1721, Russia had made considerable territorial gains and created a mighty regular army and a powerful navy.

At the beginning of the nineteenth century Russia's expansion was checked by France until Napoleon took the fateful decision to invade Russia in 1812. On this occasion the Russian army proved that it was more than a match for Europe's best army and its greatest general. Final victory, which carried the Russian army as far westwards as Paris, gave Alexander I unprecedented power and prestige.

Under the reign of Nicholas I Russia resumed her expansionist policies in the Caucasus, Persia, and against Turkey, and sent 100,000 soldiers to crush the Hungarian uprising for Austria. The industrial revolution in Europe left Russia far behind, and the army that confronted the allied forces in the Crimea was poorly armed and inadequately supplied. Reinforcements, provisions, and ammunition had to travel on dirt roads, which were often inundated, for thousands of miles, and it was estimated that only 10% of forage ever reached its destination since the other 90% had been consumed en route. Even so the 349-day siege of Sevastopol — hurriedly defended by earthworks and antiquated naval cannon — against the combined forces of France, England, Turkey, and Sardinia was no mean feat.

Alexander II instigated sweeping reforms which included the abolition of serfdom and the introduction of conscription, and in the meantime defeated Turkey. The final phase in the development of the Russian army was marked by internal unrest, and the ever widening technological gap with Western Europe.

Strength In 1900 the peace-time strength of the Russian army was estimated at 36,000 officers and 860,000 men. The mobilized strength was probably in excess of 4,000,000.

System of recruiting On 1 January 1874 the obligation of military service was imposed on all male subjects of the Russian Empire between the ages of twenty-one and forty-three. A force of 700,000 men was available for the first ballot, and the requirement was only 150,000, while by 1910 the army called up 450,000 conscripts. The remainder had to enlist in the reserve.

Terms of service Terms of service were three years active and fifteen reserve in the infantry and foot artillery, and four years and thirteen years in all other arms. Service in the reserve lasted twenty-two years. There were a number of exemptions, and postponement or curtailment was granted in exceptional cases. The only section of the population exempted from conscription were the Cossacks.

Officers Youngsters destined for military service (usually sons of officers) entered cadet school at the age of ten where they received secondary school education and basic military training. A cadet then joined a Military School for infantry, cavalry, artillery, or engineering arms. Called a Junker, he swore an oath, was subject to military discipline, and served from two to three years. On completion he was commissioned with the rank of second-lieutenant. On reaching the rank of captain he could enrol in an advanced course at an Officers' School for his particular arm. The courses lasted seven or eight months. Finally he could sit for the entrance examination to one of the six military Academies (General Staff, Artillery, Engineering, Judicial, Intendance, and Medical) where the course lasted two years.

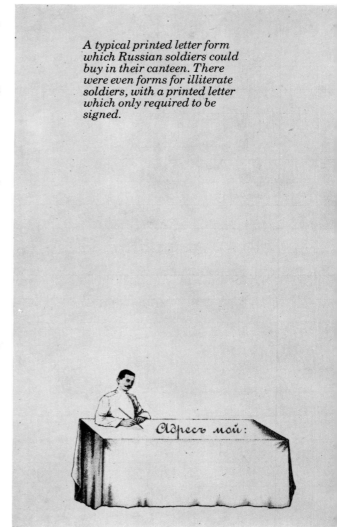

A typical printed letter form which Russian soldiers could buy in their canteen. There were even forms for illiterate soldiers, with a printed letter which only required to be signed.

Organization The army was organized into a regular army and a reserve (Opolchaniya), which was divided into two categories, infantry and artillery. Service in the first was for seven and in the second eight years, while all others served seven and six years respectively. Reserve units (Drushina) were only mobilized in wartime, and their personnel were distinguished by a cross on their head-dress.

Infantry In January 1914 there were seventeen guard and 342 line infantry regiments organized in seventy divisions and seventeen brigades. Three rifle brigades were Finnish, two Caucasian, and six from Turkestan.

Cavalry There were two guard cavalry divisions with eleven regiments, and one independent guard cavalry brigade with two regiments. Line cavalry consisted of sixteen divisions of three regular and one Cossack regiments each, three independent cavalry brigades of two regiments, and two independent regiments (20th Finnish Dragoons, and Krymski Regiment). There were three brigades of reserve cavalry.

Artillery Guard artillery included three brigades of foot artillery each with six batteries, a guard rifle artillery regiment with two batteries, and one brigade of guard horse artillery with six batteries. There were sixty-three brigades of field artillery, and sixteen division each with three batteries. In addition there were twelve horse artillery divisions of two batteries, and units of mortar, mountain, heavy and fortress artillery with supporting artillery parks.

Engineers There were forty-five battalions of engineers, two Siberian pontoon battalions, and one Turkestan pontoon company. Railway units consisted of sixteen battalions and one company.

Cossacks In theory Cossacks served all their active life. With the introduction of conscription they obtained considerable advantages because service was limited to twenty years. From the ages of eighteen to twenty-one, Cossacks went through preparatory training. From twenty-one to thirty-three they were on active service, and from thirty-three to thirty-eight in the reserve. At all times they were obliged to report for active service at a moment's notice, complete with satisfactory equipment, and approved horse provided at their own expense. The state provided only the firearms.

Geographically, Cossacks were divided into twelve armies or Voiskos under a chief or Ataman. In January 1914 the army included the following Cossack units: Tsar's Escort of two squadrons or Sotnias; one Don; one Composite; one Caucasian; one Turkestan; one Transcaspian; one West Siberian; one Transbaikal; and one Ussury cavalry brigade. Sixteen cavalry regiments were attached to line cavalry divisions; eight horse artillery divisions, and the Kuban Cossack Infantry (Plastun) Brigade of six battalions.

The vastness of the Russian fatherland has never been completely occupied by any invader. The Crimean and Russo-Japanese War defeats were harmful to Russian prestige and the internal stability of the country, but cannot be defined as defeats in the total sense. In the light of three hundred years of experience it is sufficient to say that Russian military might was numerically inexhaustible.

Above: The Tsarevitch in naval uniform with Cossack officers of his suite, 1913.

Below: Cadets of the Kazan Military School at physical training, 1914.

Right: Cavalry General Brusiloff in the uniform of the Cavalry Officers' School in 1913.

Above: Commander-in-Chief of the Russian army, Grand Duke Nicolai Nicolaievitch in 1913.

Left: Officers of the Grodno Hussars and their ladies in relaxed mood. This photograph presents a great contrast to the stiffness of the formal military portraits of the period.

Below: Russian soldiers in the first winter of World War, 1914.

5TURKEY

On 4 October 1853, eleven months before the British and French landed in the Crimea, Turkey began the Crimean War by declaring war on Russia and sending an army across the Danube into Russian-occupied Romania. Within a few weeks the Russians were driven out of Wallachia and Moldavia, back across the Pruth; the result of this campaign was a great surprise, especially in the light of the condition of the Turkish army and the character of its commander. The commander's real name was Michael Lattas. A deserter from the Austrian frontier guard, he had walked and worked his way as a carter to Constantinople, where his knowledge of several languages, his ability to read and write Turkish, and his determination to be a soldier resulted in his becoming a Moslem and a general with the name of Omar Pasha.

The army was mostly in rags, the nearest approach to a uniform being the clothing worn by the irregular troops; turbans a foot high, short braided jackets and enormous sashes around the waist, in which were carried a great assortment of weapons and ammunition. Boots were hard to come by, the usual footwear of other ranks being bundles of rags. There was no supply organization, no medical services and when, under Omar Pasha, a Turkish contingent joined the British and French in the Crimea their plight during the frightful first winter of the campaign was even worse than that of the British, for they were entirely without cold-weather clothing. This Turkish contingent was only between four and five thousand strong and signified little more than a show of inter-allied solidarity. Once the campaign in Romania was over, the main Turkish effort was concentrated in the defence of the Caucasus frontier against Russian attack. It was hard work. The poorly-clad and badly-fed Turks suffered from cold in the mountains and malaria on the coasts.

It was not until the spring of 1855, after the war had been in progress for nearly two years, that the Russians were able to make an all-out attack on Kars, the principal Turkish stronghold. During the first year of the war they had been constantly harassed and held up by guerilla forces under Shamyl, who has been described as the greatest guerilla in history. The year 1854 had been spent in a plodding advance from mountain top to mountain top, closing in on Kars where the siege finally began. In command at Kars was a British general, Sir William Fenwick Williams, who had had much experience of military missions to the Turkish army. The principal Russian assault came on 29 September. This failed with a loss of 7000 Russians, killed and wounded, but the siege went on and Williams was obliged to surrender when his food was exhausted on 26 November. Once Sevastopol was taken, Omar Pasha began collecting a Turkish force to relieve Kars, but nothing effective could be done. After the fall of Kars the next Russian objectives appeared to be Trebizond and Erzerum, and preparations were made to send a British force of 20,000 men for the defence of those places, but the war ended before the troops could be moved.

Serving with Williams in this campaign was a notable British

Opposite: A typical irregular warrior (Bashi-Bazouk) in about 1880.

A group of Turkish reservists (Redif) during the Crimean War.

soldier of fortune, Richard Guyon. Guyon had been commissioned in the Hungarian hussars at the age of twenty, married a general's daughter and, when war came between Austria and Hungary in 1848, served on the Hungarian side, being promoted general. When Hungarian resistance collapsed, he escaped to Turkey and during the war with Russia became a lieutenant general and a Pasha. Having survived the Caucasus campaign, he died of cholera at Scutari on 12 October 1856.

Williams, after his return from captivity in Russia, was created a baronet and Constable of the Tower of London, living until 1883 to enjoy these and many other distinctions.

It was not until nearly twenty years after the end of the Crimean War that a beginning was made with the reorganization of the Turkish army. In 1874 conscription was introduced, theoretically at least, but only the poor served for any length of time, even the moderately prosperous being able to buy themselves out for a sum of £50 after three months. Christians and Jews were not allowed to serve but were obliged to pay a fine. In 1910, this rule was altered and all males in the Ottoman Empire were liable for service.

German advisers were imported to take the place of the British and of the Polish and Hungarian refugees who had sought shelter in Turkey following the collapse of the independence movements in their own countries. The most important technical change was the introduction of the Peabody-Martini rifle. On the other hand, despite the really considerable impetus for reform, it never proved possible for troops' pay to be less than a year in arrears.

The first test of the reorganized army came during the brief war between Turkey and Serbia which started on 20 July 1876. The Serbs attacked but the Turks under Osman Pasha — of whom the world was to hear a great deal more — counter-attacked so

successfully that the great powers were obliged to intervene to prevent the Serbs from being overrun.

The Russians, who had supplied technical assistance of a military sort to the Serbs, then decided to carry on the struggle against Turkey and declared war on 24 April 1877. Having received Romanian permission to cross their territory, the Russians arrived at the Danube, Turkey's northern border. In a brilliant operation the Russians crossed the Danube with 150,000 men under the command of Grand Duke Nicholas, Alexander II's younger brother. Nicholas pressed south across Bulgaria towards Constantinople. Osman Pasha, who had remained near Vidin after his victory over the Serbs a year before, moved east to cut off the Russian advance. This involved a forced march of 120 miles with a column of 10,000 men, ten miles long. A breakfast of hot meat and rice was served at first light; the rest of the day's rations apparently consisted of hard biscuits, each as big as a soup plate, which had to be broken with a hatchet and soaked in water before they could be eaten.

Preceded by an advance guard of three battalions, Osman reached Plevna on 19 July. He was only just in time, for the pleasant little town, with its minarets, white houses and neat gardens, was soon the centre of one of the hardest fought battles of the nineteenth century. On the very day after Osman's arrival the Russians launched their first attack, unsuccessfully. They followed this with a bigger attack on 30 July, in which they lost 8000 men, and bringing up still more troops, on 11 September they were able to attack for the third time. This was again a very costly failure, with Russian losses of 20,000 against Turkish losses of 5000. Turkish leaders have been criticized for not following up these successes with counter-attacks. The Russians, their army now 100,000, had Plevna completely surrounded by 24 October and siege operations were begun by Todleben, who had been the chief engineer of the Russian defences at Sevastopol twenty-two years earlier. By the beginning of December, Osman decided he must fight his way out of Plevna, but he failed and was obliged to surrender on 11 December. Total losses during the siege were 38,000 Russians and 30,000 Turks. Two years after the war an English west country newspaper announced that thirty tons of human bones, comprising 3000 skeletons, had 'just been landed at Bristol from Plevna for conversion into bone meal'.

Plevna was one of the first of the great campaigns for war correspondents. Russell had been in the Crimea, American correspondents had been everywhere in the Civil War, but it was the hardier sort of correspondent who reached Plevna. Of these the best publicized was MacGahan of the London *Daily News* and the *New York Herald,* who announced himself as 'the Ambassador of the English Opposition' (i.e. Gladstone and the Liberals) and somehow got involved in a move to promote himself as head of the Bulgarian State. But the glamorous correspondents had to work. It took thirty-six hours on horseback in wild Balkan weather to reach the nearest Romanian telegraph office that had an operator capable of transmitting Latin characters, for operators in Bulgaria could only send Cyrillic characters. However, the best writing on Plevna was by F. W. von Herbert, an adventurous young man of German parentage, who was commissioned in the Turkish infantry at the age of eighteen and served through the siege, publishing his book *The Defence of Plevna* in 1895. He was later commissioned in the British army and served during the Boer War.

While the defence of Plevna was in progress, the Turks were fighting another stubborn defensive action, at the Shipka Pass on the road leading through the Balkan mountains to Adrianople and the South. From July until January 1878 the Russians, under Gourko, tried in vain to advance beyond the pass.

The Russians now resumed their march on Constantinople, which Turkish resistance had held up for six months, and reached the Chataljda lines, less than twenty miles from the Turkish capital. The British moved the Mediterranean fleet to Besika Bay at the entrance to the Dardanelles and also sent two brigades of Indian troops to Malta to act as a deterrent to a continued Russian advance. The Turks regarded the situation with a mixture of confused fears. If the Russians took Constantinople they knew very well what to expect, but on the other hand they had no confidence that if the British delivered them from the Russian evil they would then go away and leave them in peace.

During this time the Russians were again attacking in the Caucasus and once more Kars was the principal obstacle to their advance. On this occasion they realized that unlike in 1855, they could not spare the time for a six-month siege, and so decided to take the place by storm. This was done, by moonlight, on the night of 17 November 1877. The entire Turkish garrison of 24,000 was killed or taken prisoner while the Russian loss was about 2000.

When peace was signed in Berlin in July 1878, Kars was ceded to Russia and remained in Russian hands until the collapse of the Tsarist Empire. It was then reoccupied by the Turks and has remained Turkish ever since.

The Treaty of Berlin represented yet another attempt to stabilize the situation in the Balkans, brought about by the slow crumbling of the Turkish Empire. It was one of a succession of agreements: the first of which was signed in Paris in 1856; the next in Berlin in 1878; two were signed in London and Bucharest in 1912-13 after the First and Second Balkan Wars; and finally, after the First World War, another was signed in Paris. Each conference and the treaty which followed, up to the final agreement in Lausanne in 1923, registered the shrinking of Turkish territory in Europe until it consisted only of the vital bridgehead covering Adrianople, Constantinople and the Dardanelles. The final disappearance of the last of the old Turkish Empire in Asia Minor, as distinct from the Turkish heartland of Anatolia, came with the liberation of the Arab territories under the Mandates system of the League of Nations in 1919 — followed by complete independence.

Throughout the last years of Turkish rule in these areas continual guerilla campaigns were being waged by the Arabs against their overlords; and this meant that perhaps half the Turkish army at any time was tied down with counter-insurgency work. The Russian army was similarly handicapped once it was operating in unfriendly or occupied enemy territory.

In the 1890s the forces of Balkan disintegration were particularly active on the border between Greece and Turkey which, at that time, ran from Arta to Larissa. Greek irregulars, or partisans to use a later description, continually crossed the border from Greece into Turkey to stir up trouble, leading to attacks on Turkish positions. On 17 April 1897 Turkey declared war on Greece and in exactly a month the war was over. The Turkish troops were not handled with any special skill but their total strength of 58,000 men proved more than enough to deal with 45,000 Greeks, and the Turks advanced on Athens. A hasty sos was sent out by King George I of Greece to the Tsar, asking him to intercede with the Sultan and secure a cease-fire. This was arranged and the war ended.

A short war, badly handled by both sides, did not provide any special lessons. It was observed, however, that the German mission of 1883, under General von der Goltz, had considerably improved the quality of the Turkish junior officers, while the artillery, supplied by Krupp, was seen to be good and well handled, despite the fact that manoeuvrability was seriously handicapped by a lack of suitable horses.

But old customs died hard, or rather, they did not die at all. Shortly before his death in 1901, Osman Pasha discussed the charge that he was taking bribes and declared 'I do it. I openly confess it. I want all the world to know it. Perhaps when it becomes known that the defender of Plevna must cheat and steal in order to exist that iniquitous system will cease.'

In July 1908 the revolution of the 'Young Turks' took place in Constantinople. The old Sultan Abdul Hamid, 'Abdul the Damned', was eventually sent into exile and for a moment it looked as though Turkey might become a 'liberal' country. But the young and field-rank officers of the army who had taken over installed one more dictatorship, marginally more efficient than the Sultan's and perhaps better able to wage war. In October 1908 came another crack in the structure of the Turkish Empire, for the Austrians, who had been in occupation of Bosnia and Herzegovina since 1878, annexed both provinces and thus dashed the hope of the Serbs that they might soon enter into possession of them. Turkish territory, inhabited by Serbs, seemed an easier place in which to continue the liberation of the south Slav, or Yugoslav, people. The Greeks, the Bulgarians and the Montenegrins were similarly eager to take advantage of what seemed to be the imminent collapse of Turkey and, with enormous labour, an alliance of Bulgaria, Greece, Montenegro and Serbia was constructed. The great difficulty was that Greece, Serbia and Bulgaria all claimed territories now Turkish which had previously belonged to them, and this they could not forget when they made wide claims for the division of the spoils

after a victorious war. Nevertheless, thanks largely to the patience
and diplomacy of J. D. Bourchier, the principal corespondent of *The
Times* in the Balkans, the Balkan League against Turkey was
formed. While negotiations for it were under way, a dispute between
Turkey and Italy came to a head.

Turkey had once controlled the entire North African shore from
the Red Sea to the Atlantic, but by 1911 all that remained was
Libya, which the Italians were engaged in developing, more from
the point of view of colonial prestige than from that of commercial
prosperity. The Italian government, though in those days a
parliamentary democracy, acted with the same brutality that
characterized Mussolini a quarter of a century later. Rome
complained that her development plans were being interfered with
and demanded that Turkey yield Libya to her; the Turks refused
and the Italians sent an expeditionary force to seize the colony. It
was in this war that aeroplanes were used for the first time. To the
surprise of the world, the Turks would not surrender, but withdrew
into the interior of the country and, with the support of the Arab
population, kept up a guerilla struggle, in places whose names were
to be celebrated thirty years later — Tobruk, Benghazi, Tripoli,
Derna. They were so successful that when the First World War
broke out the Italians still held only four small bridgeheads along
the coast, although peace between Italy and Turkey had been

*Above: General Liman von
Sanders (fourth from left)
with his staff of instructors.*

*Left: The Turkish Minister of
War, Riza Pasha, 1896.*

concluded on 15 October 1912, at Ouchy. Turkey surrendered Libya and following this Turkish reverse, mid-October saw a flurry of declarations of war. Montenegro declared war on Turkey, who replied by declaring war on Bulgaria and Serbia on 17 October. Greece declared war on Turkey the following day, thus completing the series, which had been spread over just ten days.

The Turkish army was divided into two portions, one in Thrace 226,000 strong, and the other in Macedonia numbering 140,000, of which, however, no more than 50,000 were ever assembled in one place. The reason for this division of forces was the fact that the Greeks had command of the sea, thanks to their possession of the only large modern ship on either side. Events now moved so fast that the war was over before the Turkish mobilization was completed.

Of the allies Bulgaria had 280,000 men, Serbia 450,000, Greece 110,000 and Montenegro 47,000. From the first days of the war the great weakness of the alliance was the inability of its members to agree on the conduct of the war and the division of the spoils.

The Bulgarians, having agreed to help the Serbs in Macedonia, withdrew two of their three promised divisions at the last moment and concentrated their efforts on Constantinople, while the one division left in Macedonia ignored the enemy and headed for Salonika with the hope of getting there before the Greeks. In fact they were beaten by one day. The rest of the Greek army advanced

Below: Mounted band of the Ertogorul Regiment in the streets of Constantinople, c. 1900. This regiment carried out ceremonial duties in the capital.

Overleaf: Officers and men of the 1st Lancer Regiment.

Opposite: Men of the 1st Brigade of the Pera Artillery Regiment at gun drill, 1896.

northward and besieged the town of Janina in Epirus. Meanwhile the Bulgarians, having won a notable victory over the Turks at Lule Burgas, invested Adrianople and pressed on to the Chataljda lines, which once again stood between the Turkish capital and the invader. The Serbians also won an important victory, at Kumanovo, and on 3 December the Turks agreed to an armistice with Bulgaria, Serbia, and Montenegro. Greece, however, refused to sign, and the Greek army continued the siege of Janina. A peace conference was called in London but agreement was impossible. The war was resumed on 3 February 1913 and the sieges of Adrianople and Janina were successfully concluded by the allies. Negotiations were continued and a peace treaty was signed on 30 May. This peace lasted exactly a month. The Bulgarians, dissatisfied with their share of the spoils, launched a surprise attack on their allies but were immediately defeated. Romania intervened with an invasion of Bulgaria and occupied the southernmost part of the province of the Dobrudja, while the Turks came back into the war to re-take Adrianople, which had fallen to the Bulgarians on 26 March.

During the autumn and winter of 1913-14, peace treaties were signed between the various belligerents. But peace in the Balkans was to last only until the declaration of war by Austro-Hungary on Serbia on 28 July 1914, following the assassination of the Archduke Francis Ferdinand. Turkey was soon involved and on 29 October Turkish forces committed acts of war against Russia in the Black Sea and against Britain in the Sinai.

Immediately after the Balkan Wars had ended the German general Liman von Sanders was appointed to reorganize the Turkish army. He was able to replace much of the artillery which Turkey had lost but there was not much that he or the other German officers serving with him could do to overcome shortages, corruption and ignorance. Thus in 1914 95% of Turkish other ranks were illiterate and according to a German instructor, even some Turkish officers on the staff were unable to read or write. This same authority described the Turkish soldier as 'steadfast, self-sufficient and patient'.

The outbreak of war in 1914 was a bad time for prophets. In respect of the Turkish army, few were as mistaken as Sir Henry Wilson, later Chief of the Imperial General Staff, who said in 1914: 'The Turkish is not a serious modern army — ill-commanded, ill-officered and in rags.' This belief was one of the reasons why the allies thought, in the following year, that they would be able to force the Dardanelles. But when the attempt had been made and failed, Sir Ian Hamilton, the Allied Commander-in-Chief, giving evidence before the Dardanelles Commission appointed to enquire into the failure of the expedition, said of the Turkish troops: 'I did not know, to tell you the truth, that they were nearly as good as they turned out to be.'

Long after the campaign was over a popular saying still went the rounds — the ideal army would have Turkish privates, British NCOs and Australian officers.

TURKEY

History and traditions Until their extermination in 1826 the Janissaries were the dominant military force in Turkey. Their departure signalled the end of the old Turkish army and the beginning of the reforms designed to create a new force on the Western model. It was not, however, until 1843 that regular service in the active army (Nizam) and the reserve army (Redif) was instituted. Reorganization followed the wars of 1854 and 1878 against Russia, and the army gradually began to progress along modern lines. The Turkish army saw considerable active service in the nineteenth century, and in spite of failures in administration and supply the Turkish soldier proved a formidable fighter, particularly in defence.

Strength The mobilized strength of the Turkish army in 1904 was estimated at 1,795,350 men from all categories both trained and untrained. The active army totalled 230,408 men.

System of recruiting On the advice of General von der Goltz, who had been seconded to the Turkish War Office, a territorial system of organization and recruitment was introduced in 1886. The army was recruited solely from orthodox Mohammedans while other religious sects were excluded on payment of a military tax.

Terms of service Liability for service was from the age of twenty to the age of forty for all Ottoman male subjects. Active service totalled nine years, of which three years in the case of the infantry and four years in that of the cavalry and artillery were spent with the colours. Service in the reserve of the active army (Ikhtiat) was divided into six and five years respectively, after which men passed into the Landwehr (Redif) for nine years, and finally into territorial service (Mustahfiz) for two years.

Organization The army was divided into seven army corps (Ordus) and the independent commands of Tripoli and the Hedjaz. The corps headquarters were Constantinople, Adrianople, Salonika, Erzerum, Damascus, Bagdad, and Yemen.

Infantry The infantry establishment in 1904 was given as seventy-nine Nizam regiments of four battalions, and twenty-four Chasseur battalions. In addition the reserve categories provided approximately 540 battalions of infantry.

Cavalry The cavalry comprised one guard regiment, two hussar regiments, and thirty-eight Nizam regiments. The later served as cavalry brigades attached to the first six army corps, while the twelve regiments of reserve cavalry were employed as divisional troops in time of war. In 1904 the total cavalry strength was 1580 officers and 26,800 men.

Artillery The artillery formed an independent command consisting solely of Nizam troops with an establishment of 198 field batteries (1188 guns), twelve howitzer batteries (72 guns), eighteen horse batteries (108 guns) and forty mountain batteries (240 guns).

German participation in the modernization of the Turkish army had begun in 1882, and it was to continue until the end of the First World War. With this aid the Turks had achieved much, but their efforts were hampered by the nation's lack of sophisticated technology, by its inadequate system of communications, and by the poverty of its people. The prime resource of the Turkish army remained its manpower which was hardy, courageous, and indomitable.

Napoleon I was not only a foster father of the political unification of Italy but also the provider of the means by which that unification could be achieved and maintained, for it was under his command that Italian troops had learned to fight well. They in turn supplied him with a good proportion of his more competent senior officers.

After Waterloo almost all traces of Napoleon's reforms in Italy disappeared except that the kingdom of Sardinia (also referred to as Piedmont) emerged possessor of a small but efficient army, which was to play a most important part in the events of the next half-century, and especially of the two decades between 1848 and 1870. This period was to witness the realization of Italian unity despite the fact that it began disastrously for the Italians in general and the Sardinians in particular. In 1848 the people of Milan, then an Austrian possession, rose against the garrison. The first sign of discontent was a boycott of tobacco, the Austrian monopoly of which was an important source of the government's revenue. Rioting broke out, and the people of Milan, together with those of Venice, where similar riots were in progress, appealed to the Sardinians and their King, Charles Albert, for aid. Popular opinion in the territories of Sardinia enthusiastically accepted the call and Sardinian troops moved to liberate Milan. It was, however, to be a liberation of short duration, for the Austrians under Radetzky counter-attacked, defeated Charles Albert at the first battle of Custozza on 25 July 1848, and retook the territory which they had lost. Peace followed, to be broken after only nine months, by the second Austro-Sardinian War which lasted less than a week. The Italians were beaten again, at Novara on 23 March 1849, on this occasion under the command of a Polish general, Krzanowski.

Charles Albert abdicated and was succeeded by his son, Victor Emmanuel, who was offered generous peace terms by Austria on two conditions; first, that he abandon the red, white, and green tricolour, a legacy of Napoleon's kingdom of Italy; and second, that he repeal the constitution of his country which had just been granted by Charles Albert at the insistence of his subjects. Victor Emmanuel refused the Austrian terms but the French government intervened to prevent the imposition of a vengeful peace, and Victor Emmanuel, with Cavour as his Prime Minister, was well on his way to becoming the first king of a united Italy.

At the same time two other Italian insurrections against the status quo were defeated. Garibaldi's attempt to form a Roman Republic failed in the face of French intervention and a rising in Venice was put down in a series of operations which involved the first air-raid in history, balloons carrying bombs being launched from the decks of an Austrian fleet blockading the port. No damage was done.

The next move by Sardinia was to offer troops to the Franco-British alliance in the Crimean War. The offer was accepted gratefully, especially by the British who had prompted it in the first place and were, as usual, short of troops. The prospect of an additional 15,000 men was acceptable to Britain and France for another reason. Both countries were hoping to persuade Austria to join them in their war against Russia; this Austria hesitated to do, for she feared that, should she concentrate her troops against Russia on her northern and eastern frontiers, she would be attacked in the south-west by the Sardinians. However, if one quarter of the total Sardinian army was fighting in the Black Sea it seemed unlikely that the remainder would attack Austria at the same time. Although the Sardinian troops sailed to the Crimea, the Austrians did not declare war on Russia and contented themselves with a benevolent neutrality towards the allies until peace-talks began, when they put pressure on Russia to sign the treaty ending the war. The treaty was duly signed in Paris on 30 March 1856.

As for the Sardinians in the Crimea, they took part in the battle of Tchernaya on 15 August 1855 under General La Marmora, and were held to have done well, helping the French to repel a major Russian attack designed to take the allied forces besieging Sevastopol in the rear. Like all the other armies in this campaign, and in most campaigns of pre-1914 days, they suffered much heavier losses from disease than from enemy action.

Cavour continued his preparations for the war of 1859 at the side of the French. When it came, the Sardinians fielded their full strength of 60,000 men and played an important part in the two victories over the Austrians at Magenta (4 June) and Solferino (24 June). The battlefield of Solferino had only recently been used by the Austrians for large-scale exercises and trenches dug then still survived to serve in the real battle. The position of the Sardinians was on the left of the allied line on the shores of Lake Garda, where they fought all day, in summer heat and a tropical rain storm, to take the village of San Martino, held by the Austrian VIII Corps under Benedek. Finally, after a long day, when the rest of the Austrian army had drawn off, Benedek too withdrew.

The principal technical lesson of these two battles was that the French breech-loading rifled guns were greatly superior to the muzzle-loaders of the Austrian artillery.

Napoleon now decided to bring to an end the war which he had begun only a few weeks before. Sardinia was obliged publicly to follow suit but, in fact, under Garibaldi's leadership prepared to carry on the struggle for Italian unification. For the time being the target was shifted from Austria to the kingdom of Naples (also called the kingdom of the Two Sicilies). Garibaldi, returning from the exile imposed on him for his failure to protect the Roman Republic from French troops in 1849, enlisted a body of a thousand volunteers and sailed with them for Sicily, wearing the picturesque red shirts which had been originally intended for slaughter-house workers. Landing at Marsala on 11 May 1860, he defeated the Neapolitan forces at Calatafimi on 15 May, picked up about a thousand fresh volunteers from the surrounding countryside, and went on to Milazzo. He defeated another army there on 20 July and crossing over onto the toe of the mainland of Italy, he then advanced on Naples where by now resistance had almost completely collapsed. The capture of Naples was easy, and the King of Naples, Francis II, and what was left of his army withdrew into the fortress of Gaeta. Gaeta could clearly only be taken by siege and Garibaldi's force was not equipped for this. Accordingly, on 3 November an officer of the regular Sardinian army, Colonel Cialdini, took over command from the entirely irregular Garibaldi, giving the Red Shirts something of an air of respectability. This move was timely, for most European governments were in a state of alarm lest Garibaldi continue his brilliantly successful campaign with a dash for Rome. If Rome were to fall, Napoleon would incur the displeasure of French right-wing opinion and could lose his throne. To prevent this, he sent troops to Rome. In addition to the French troops there was formed for the defence of Rome an international force of Catholic volunteers; French, Belgian, Dutch and Swiss soldiers, known as the Papal Zouaves.

During the siege of Gaeta a French squadron lay off the port, in theory neutral, but making it impossible by their presence for the Italians to attack the port from the sea or to blockade it. However, at the beginning of 1861 the French ships were withdrawn, and Gaeta fell. Rome, the supreme goal of all Italian patriots, was again threatened, though it was not to fall for another nine years. Nevertheless, most of the territories of the Papal States were now included in the newly constituted kingdom of Italy, with its capital at Florence.

Cavour died in 1861 but Victor Emmanuel and his new Prime Minister, Ricasoli, found a new, if temporary ally who would give them the support which Napoleon had now withdrawn. This was Prussia, on the verge of the Seven Weeks War against Austria and some of the lesser German states. Politically the Italian decision was wise enough, for the Prussians were sure to win and, in consequence, Italy would receive Venice as a reward for drawing a proportion of the Austrian army down to the Italian front. But to fight successfully, the Italians had to have an efficient army, and this did not exist. The former Sardinian army, 60,000 strong and known for its efficiency, had been merged into an Italian army of 450,000, of whom 270,000 took the field in 1866. The quality of the whole force had suffered greatly, for it was a mixture of several armies of small states, some of which had, a short time previously, been at war with each other. Mobilization took time; the Prussians were ready within three weeks, the Austrians took seven or eight weeks, but there were only 80,000 Italians available when, with La Marmora in command, they advanced into Austrian-held territory and met the Austrian army under Archduke Albrecht at Custozza, eleven miles southwest of Verona. The town had already been the scene of one victory of the Austrians over the Italians when, in 1848, Radetzky defeated Charles Albert's army, driving it out of Lombardy. History now repeated itself, but before the Austrians could exploit this success the Prussians had won the battle of Sadowa on 3 July. Francis Joseph had already agreed to cede Venice to Italy, thus removing the Italian danger to his rear, so that the second battle of Custozza had been entirely unnecessary. Today it is odd to observe that the campaigns in northern Italy in 1859 and 1866 had been intended by the Austrians as merely token resistance. Neither was maintained for more than a few weeks and both ended in the Austrians yielding the territory which was in dispute, as they had always intended to do.

Napoleon now announced his intention of mediating and he asked Prussia and Italy to cease hostilities; they both refused to do this until agreement on terms had been reached. The Italians paid for their refusal by having their fleet defeated by the Austrians off the island of Lissa in the Adriatic.

Peace negotiations lasted nearly as long as the war. Prussia and Austria reached agreement easily enough as Bismarck asked neither for reparations nor territory, all that he had wished for had been Austria's promise not to interfere in Germany. The Italians had been extremely interested spectators of these negotiations. For they hoped that, while the Austrians were still occupied with the Prussians, it would be possible to seize the Trentino, one of the last Austrian-held territories inhabited by people of Italian race.

There was little time to be spent regretting this lost opportunity for, almost immediately, Italian troops were engaged in battle with Garibaldi who, regardless of the effects of his plans on the rickety balance of European power, now made another attempt to take Rome. His plan called for the formation of a private army about 30,000 strong, with which he would attack the Papal forces, while inside Rome the population would rise against the government. If he were able to defeat the Roman troops then everything would be concentrated against the capital. The preparations for this seem to have been made at least semi-publicly, and Napoleon learned what was in the wind in plenty of time to replace his garrison in Rome, which he had withdrawn the previous year. The French army and the Catholic volunteers fought well. The Garibaldini were easily defeated and Garibaldi was wounded and taken prisoner.

It was now necessary to wait for nearly three years for the final fall of Rome. Napoleon's defeat at Sedan meant that there could be no interference with Italian plans by France and on 20 September 1870, Italian troops commanded by General Cadorna entered the city down the street which now bears as its name this historic date. There was little fighting and soon a white flag could be seen flying from the top of the dome of St Peter's.

Italy was at last a whole nation, poor yet ambitious. It was obvious that she required a navy as well as an army, for she was almost as dependent on the sea for her trade as Britain. She also decided that she needed a colonial empire.

Meanwhile there had been the problem of forming an army out of the forces of the small countries which were now legally one but whose population was composed of so very many diverse elements. The method used to deal with this problem, which may not have been the best and which was certainly not entirely successful, was to mix men from all over Italy and place these 'mixes' in the same

Right: Distribution of daily rations to the 74th Infantry Regiment at Syracuse, 1898.

Below: A Bersaglieri (rifle) battalion in 1899.

Below: Cyclists of the 9th Bersaglieri, 1899.

Opposite: Bersaglieri also formed part of the international force in Peking in 1900.

units. It did not begin by encouraging comradeship. A continuing cause for complaint amongst the other ranks of the Italian army was one that stemmed from the geography of the country. The situation in Europe was such that the great bulk of the army had to be stationed in the north, opposite the frontiers of France and Austria, for both countries seemed to be potential enemies. But the troops stationed in the north consisted not only of those whose homes were in the area but also soldiers from the south. When these men went on leave they were faced with two long rail journeys and many accordingly complained.

The 'mixes' of troops also made difficult the organization of depots. After the Franco-Prussian War, it was admitted that the ideal system was to keep troops and reservists of the same unit together in the same neighbourhood, but the whole principle of the Italian scheme was to have units composed of men from all parts of the kingdom. Accordingly, on mobilization, reservists called to the colours had to make their different ways individually all over the country, just as the French reservists had done at the outbreak of the Franco-Prussian War. However, the consequences of this were not as disastrous for the Italian army as they had been for the French, for a period of some nine months intervened between Italian mobilization in July and August 1914 and the Italian declaration of war on 23 May of the following year.

The unification of Italy was achieved just in time for the new country to take, belatedly, a small share in the division of Africa. In

Italy's case the flag followed trade; the Rubattino Steamship Company, trading between Italy and the Far East, established in 1870 a coaling base at Assab, in what is now Eritrea.

In 1882 Assab was taken over by the Italian government, as was Massawa in 1885, when the area was opened up by the collapse of the empire of the Khedive of Egypt. Egyptian forces had occupied Harrar, Kassala, Massawa and the northern coast of Somalia to its furthest tip at Cape Guardafui. The Mahdi's rising in the Sudan had cut all land communications between Egypt and its distant possessions to the south, so that Egyptian troops had to be withdrawn, creating a vacuum of which Italy and Abyssinia both took advantage. At this time the Italians began occupying ports on the east coast of Somaliland, which had belonged more or less legally to the Sultan of Zanzibar.

A confrontation now developed between Italy and Abyssinia, as the Italians worked their way up the high escarpment at the top of which are Asmara and the vast plateau stretching right across Abyssinia. A treaty between Rome and Addis Ababa followed, but the interpretation of the agreement led directly to the dispute which it was designed to avoid. The Italian text spoke of the Abyssinian Emperor, Menelek, agreeing to be guided by Italian advice in his conduct of foreign affairs, while the Amharic text merely said that he might be so guided.

The French government was quick to take advantage of this, explaining to Menelek how he had been tricked and arranging a

deal with the Abyssinian government whereby France supplied arms and ammunition in exchange for mules which the French required for their campaign in Madagascar.

Early in 1895 the Abyssinians decided to try their new weapons against the Italians and, after being checked at the battle of Coatit, gathered a great force of 100,000 men. Using part of this force, they won two minor victories, at Amba Alagi on 7 December 1895 and at Makalle on 23 January 1896. Menelek then offered to make peace and released the prisoners that he had taken.

The Italian government under Francesco Crispi who, more than anyone else, had been responsible for the latest moves of colonial policy, ordered General Baratieri to refuse the proffered peace and to continue the war until the Italian defeats had been avenged. Menelek by now had taken up a strong position in the hills around Adowa with about 120,000 men while Baratieri faced him with a mixed force of about 25,000, of whom 10,000 were Italian and the rest Africans with Italian officers. Supplies were very difficult to obtain for both sides, and Baratieri was obliged to decline further reinforcements as he could not feed them.

Crispi now intervened again, ordering Baratieri to advance and at the same time secretly sending another general, Antonio Baldissera, to supersede him. Baratieri learned of this move from friends in Rome and decided to attack before Baldissera could reach Eritrea. On 1 March 1896 the advancing Italian brigades, supplied with poor maps and bad guides, soon lost their way in the wild and mountainous country. Endeavouring to fall back, they found that there were now some 30,000 enemy in position to cut off their retreat. In all the Abyssinians are believed to have lost 7000 killed and 10,000 wounded, while the Italian troops, white and black, lost nearly 10,000 killed and wounded out of 17,000. Later it was established that if Baratieri had remained in his position for a few days longer, Menelek would have withdrawn and the catastrophe of Adowa would never have occurred. A by-product of this battle was the decision by the British government to order the reconquest of the Sudan by the Anglo-Egyptian army under Kitchener.

By 1908 the financial state of Italy and the drain upon her young manpower due to the attractions of emigration had brought the army to the lowest level of any of the principal European conscript forces. Yet in 1911-12 the Italian army invaded another vast area. The Italian government suddenly presented Turkey with an ultimatum, demanding the right to occupy the territory now known as Libya. It was an ill-planned venture, both politically and militarily. Politically it was unwise because Germany and Austria, Italy's fellow members of the Triple Alliance, would not let her operate against Turkey in Europe (which, in this context, meant the Dardanelles) or attack the Turkish fleet. On the military side the small Turkish forces in Libya, aided by the Senussi, kept the struggle going for a year and, when war broke out in 1915, the Italians found themselves shut up in the four ports of Derna, Benghazi, Misurata and Tripoli, with neither plans nor material for an effective campaign.

ITALY

History and traditions Although as a nation Italy has only existed since 1861 the traditions of many of its finest regiments date from the seventeenth century. The Italian infantry traces its origins to the guard regiments created by Charles Emmanuel, Duke of Savoy in 1664, while the cavalry descends from the Piedmontese regiments of Emmanuel Philibert. The early nineteenth century saw the formation of the Carabinieri in 1814 and the Bersaglieri in 1836. The Bersaglieri were established by Alessandro Evasio Ferrero, Marquis of La Marmora, as a select corps of sharpshooters, and in the interval between the wars of Independence they fought alongside the British and the French in the Crimea. The need to defend Italy's mountainous frontiers led to the creation in 1872 of the Alpini, a corps of troops skilled in mountaineering and survival at extreme altitude. These premier regiments of the army were both an expression and a guarantee of Italy's hard-won unity, and the strength of their national commitment was shown repeatedly during the fierce battles of the First World War.

Strength The peace establishment of the active army was 222,000 officers and men but in war the field army could dispose of a strength of 738,000. Although not immediately available on mobilization, the territorial and mobile militias would eventually increase the war establishment to a total of 3,325,000 men.

Terms of service Liability for service in the army occurred between the ages of twenty and thirty-nine and it was divided amongst the standing army, the mobile militia and the territorial militia. A high proportion of recruits were exempted from active service but were expected to remain in the territorial militia for nineteen years. The remainder drew lots, and those selected for the first category served three years in the active army, five years in the reserve, and eleven years in the militia. The second category spent eight years in the reserve and eleven years in the militia.

Officers The majority of the officer corps was supplied by the military schools of Milan, Florence, Rome, Naples and Messina, and by the higher schools of Modena and Turin. Approximately one-third of the officers were promoted from the ranks.

Organization The country was divided into twelve military districts each providing an army corps of two infantry divisions, one cavalry regiment, two regiments of field artillery, and supporting troops.

Infantry In 1900 the regiments forming the twenty-four infantry divisions included twelve of Bersaglieri and seven of Alpini. Every regiment had three battalions, each of four companies.

Cavalry The small cavalry establishment comprised twenty-four regiments, ten of lancers and fourteen light cavalry, containing six squadrons and a depot.

Artillery The artillery consisted of twenty-four field regiments, one regiment of horse artillery, one regiment of mountain artillery, and three regiments of garrison artillery.

Mobile militia The mobile militia represented the second line of the reserve and it contained fifty-one line regiments, twenty battalions of Bersaglieri, thirty-eight companies of Alpini, thirty-one squadrons of cavalry, seventy-eight batteries and seventy-eight companies of artillery, and fifty-four engineer companies.

Territorial militia The territorial militia, representing the third line of the reserve, could call upon a numerical strength of 324 battalions of infantry, twenty-two battalions of Alpini and 100 fortress artillery companies, but in terms of active service at least 60% of these troops were completely untrained.

Despite Italy's colonial campaigns in Abyssinia and Tripolitania her army by 1914 still lacked adequate practical experience of modern warfare, and there were serious deficiencies in the provision of heavy and automatic weapons and in the mobilization and training of manpower.

G. R.

Queen's Own Hussars.

WANTED

FOR THAT

Celebrated Regiment the 7th. or Queen's own Hussars,

COMMANDED BY THAT GALLANT OFFICER, LIEUT. GENERAL

HENRY LORD PAGET,

A few handsome young men, who are anxious to distinguish themselves in defence of their King and Country; which they will have an opportunity of doing within a short period, as the Regiment-being now nearly complete, will certainly be soon employed.

The Character of the Regiment is too well known to need any comment, on service it has invariably met the Enemy and defeated them; at home it is in every quarter a favourite.

A Soldier's Life in this Corps is a continued series of pleasure.

Punishment is totally Unknown,

WHILST

EVERY POSSIBLE INDULGENCE IS GRANTED.

LIEUT. FRASER regrets extremely that he is prevented from offering

A BOUNTY of ONE HUNDRED GUINEAS,

But the highest allowed will be given by applying to him at LANGTON, or SERJEANT ROSS at the RED LION INN, BLANDFORD.

The Party will remain but a short time in this quarter, any young men desirous of enlisting are requested to apply without delay.

GOD SAVE THE KING.

The BRINGER of a Recruit shall receive the Sum of THREE GUINEAS on being finally approved of.

A late Georgian recruiting broadsheet. Although a little early for this particular work, it does illustrate the sort of 'sales patter' that recruiting sergeants of the Victorian period would have used.

1 UNITED KINGDOM

In the spring of 1854, forty years after the end of the Peninsular War, a British army once again went to war with a European power. Clad in the brilliant scarlet and gold uniforms, almost identical with those worn in the long struggle against France, and commanded by a veteran officer who had served in Spain and at Waterloo on the staff of Wellington, the army landed in the Crimea to fight the Russians. Two years later what was left of that army returned to England, having sustained casualties totalling 90% of the original contingent of 25,000 men. The greater proportion of these losses were due, not to the eleven-month Russian defence of Sevastopol, but to 'overwork, exposure to wet and cold, improper food, insufficient clothing, during part of the winter, and insufficient shelter', to quote the conclusions of the enquiry which had been appointed to consider the causes of the great Crimean disaster. The services, which are necessary to an efficient army, had been abolished in the interests of economy and as a result there were no adequate medical services, supply services or transport. With handicaps like these it would have been very nearly impossible for any army to wage war two thousand miles from home on a bleak, unfriendly coast with sweltering summers and savage winters, and a foe who was hardy and numerous. There was, in addition, a characteristic of the British army at this time which was very much more serious, and which indeed proved very nearly fatal. Briefly, the officers were terribly ignorant and, for reasons which went back two hundred years in English history, there was no one both willing and able to rectify this state of affairs. The upper classes, who ruled the country and provided the money for the upkeep of the army, had, incredibly, a great fear of the consequences of creating an efficient army, for they believed that, if the Sovereign had at his disposal such a force, he would be able to establish absolute authority over Parliament. This seems ridiculous now, but in 1816 it did not seem ridiculous to Lord Liverpool, the Prime Minister, when he criticized the proposal to found a club for serving officers on the ground that it would appear that the army was establishing an officer caste outside the rest of the community. Nevertheless, a caste system did develop out of the extremely narrow circle which supplied the officers. Officers could only be drawn from the monied classes because Parliament would never vote enough money to make soldiering a career in which it was possible for an officer to live on his pay.

In addition there was a general feeling, which is still not quite dead, that it was 'not done' to appear to be too keen or to work too hard. Coupled with this was a system which gave frequent, very extended leaves, lasting months at a time and mostly spent in sporting activities at home or overseas.

Private soldiers were recruited from the most miserable sections of the people. For some years a large proportion of private soldiers were Irish, fleeing from famine. When emigration got under way, however, Parliament had to make an effort to attract recruits, and there began a slow improvement in standards. But there remained among the more prosperous members of the working classes and the lower middle class a prejudice against the army and the career of a soldier which only the First World War was to dissipate entirely. This late Victorian attitude was an injustice against which Kipling's romantic spirit protested with all the power at his command.

In these unpromising circumstances the post-Crimean British army was formed. Its other ranks were hardy, brave and well-disciplined, led by officers with the same characteristics, but with little imagination or knowledge of their profession. From the Crimean War to 1914 a process went on from which emerged qualitatively the finest army of those days, but it all took a very long time. Conservatism, vested interests, and what seemed sheer obstinacy formed a kind of slough through which the army dragged itself — as it was to drag itself through the slough of trench warfare.

The pyramid of the almost monolithic mass of resistance to change was capped by the Commander-in-Chief of the Army, H.R.H. the Duke of Cambridge, a cousin of Queen Victoria who, with her support, held his post from 1856 until 1895, despite attempts to dislodge him. But progress was made; the higher education of officers was attended to by creating a Staff College at Camberley. Officers' career prospects were much improved, as was their efficiency by the abolition of the system of purchase whereby a man of means in the infantry or cavalry might make his way up the Army List by buying each step until he arrived at a colonelcy, when he became virtual proprietor of his regiment.

For other ranks a twelve-year period of enlistment was introduced divided between service with the colours and in the reserve, periods varying according to the needs of the army and, wherever possible, the wishes of the soldier. At this time a general rise in the standard of living also began to produce a better class of recruit.

As the British Empire spread, so the responsibilities of the army spread with it, and it became necessary to set up a regular system providing for overseas garrisons with reinforcements in case of need. To do this infantry battalions were organized in pairs, becoming the 1st and 2nd battalions of a regiment which, as far as possible, was given the name of the county or counties in which it had usually been recruited. Of these pairs of linked battalions, one was usually at home, while the other was overseas, kept up to strength by drafts from the home-based unit. At the same time local

Opposite above: Early amphibious operations: British troops landing in the Crimea in 1854.

Below: Men of the 95th Foot who had distinguished themselves during the Crimean War. They wear the recently introduced tunic, 1855.

volunteer and militia units, part-time soldiers, were attached to the regiment as additional battalions, so that the training of all troops could be carried out on uniform lines.

Most of these reforms were instigated by the Secretary for War, Cardwell. He was able to carry them through as a result of military developments in Europe following the rise of a united Germany. The idea that Britain might once again become involved in military operations in Europe, or indeed that Britain might actually be invaded, began slowly to appear a possibility. Whatever happened, there would still remain the need to garrison territories all around the world.

A bare list of the campaigns fought by the British and Indian armies between the end of the Crimean War in 1856 and the beginning of the Second Boer War in 1899 gives a clear idea of the vast commitments of the army at a time when, in theory, the country was at peace.

The Indian Mutiny in 1857-9 was the biggest challenge that the British army had to face until 1914. The Indian army was rent in two, but the Mutiny had been put down by British and Indian troops fighting side by side against the mutineers. The Indian army and the British army in India fought almost continual campaigns to maintain order on the frontiers of India. In 1856 there had been an expedition to Persia, with landings at Bushire and in the Tigris Delta. This compelled the Persians to evacuate Herat, from where they were threatening an invasion — believed to be Russian-inspired — of Afghanistan.

During 1859 and 1860 there were joint Anglo-French campaigns in China, the Western powers being anxious to force their goods on the enormous Chinese market. Unfortunately, amongst the items which the West wished to sell was opium, banned in China. In any event the Chinese authorities were well satisfied by the manner in which the centuries had passed without contact between their country and the rest of the world. In 1859 the allies occupied Canton, and then attacked the forts at Taku at the mouth of the Peiho River, leading to Peking. A British landing was defeated here on 25 June 1859, but in the following year the allies attacked once more. The vast mud flats on the river's edge were a most serious obstacle, but the allies succeeded in storming the forts on the shore. One British brigade and its commanding brigadier advanced to the attack with their trousers, socks and boots dangling from swords and rifles, where they had been tied to prevent them from getting muddy. After the capture of Taku the allies advanced on Peking where the French sacked the Imperial palace and terms of peace were dictated.

Between 1863 and 1870 the army and the navy were involved in fighting between the settlers and the Maoris, on the North Island of New Zealand, to the south of Auckland. Major E. W. Sheppard, the British military historian, has written of the Maoris that they were 'perhaps the ablest and certainly the most chivalrous of all the savage races who have ever in the various quarters of the globe measured themselves against us'. Maori arms consisted of spears,

Opposite: Recruiting sergeants gather outside the 'Mitre and Dove' in Westminster, 1875.

axes, clubs and shotguns, but this very limited technology was backed by forts called *pahs* and trench systems practically invulnerable to the available artillery, and so well sited as to necessitate a direct assault which could be costly and often unsuccessful. They had a simple view of warfare; they complained that the British would not stop fighting on Sunday, and when their own ammunition was exhausted they applied to the British for more. Finally investment and starvation brought about their surrender.

In 1867 an expedition was mounted to rescue a number of European hostages seized by Theodore, Emperor of Abyssinia. The hostages were rescued; the Emperor committed suicide; and the British army withdrew. Its casualties had been low and the affair was chiefly noteworthy because of the very successful logistic arrangements for the advance through 400 miles of mountainous country. Writing of the campaign Sir John Fortescue, in his *History of the British Army,* remarks that 'the principal difficulty was not to beat the enemy but to reach him'.

In 1870 there followed another campaign which depended for its success upon brilliant logistics and which brought to the fore an officer who for years was described by the British public as 'our only general' and whose name became a by-word for efficiency — Sir Garnet Wolseley, celebrated by W. S. Gilbert in the song 'I am the very model of a modern Major-General'.

As part of the final phase of the organization of the Dominion of Canada the lands of the Hudson's Bay Company were incorporated in the new Dominion, despite the violent opposition of the half-breeds and French Canadians in the territory, who feared for the loss of their irregular way of life. Led by Louis Riel, himself a half-breed, the dissidents seized Fort Garry and, after they had committed various acts of violence including murder, the Canadian government decided to suppress the movement. This involved sending some 1200 troops (400 British and the rest Canadian) under Wolseley from Toronto to the scene of the trouble, a distance of 1000 miles. The railway was soon left behind, and lake steamers, sleighs, canoes and barges were used, altogether a fleet of 150 boats. It was a superb feat of organization. The rebellion collapsed without further loss of life and Riel fled to the United States, to reappear some fifteen years later to start another rebellion. This was put down by Canadian troops who captured Riel, tried and hanged him.

Throughout these years war was endemic in West Africa and Wolseley again did well, his powers of organization in the campaign of 1873-4 making it possible to conclude operations before the beginning of the rainy season. These campaigns in West Africa were almost all carried out by African troops.

At the same time as these operations were in progress, campaigns were being fought in South Africa, first against Kaffirs and Zulus and then against the Boers. A British attempt to disarm the Zulus, who were a continual threat to the peace of the white settlers and the rest of the African population, was checked in January 1879 by the Zulu victory at Isandlhwana. In this battle 1800 British soldiers

Captured guns at Kabul during the second Afghan War, 1879.

were overwhelmed by 20,000 Zulus armed solely with assegais (throwing spears), and only fifty-five British escaped alive. On the same day another force of Zulus, 4000 strong, attacked an outpost of 140 British troops at Rorke's Drift. After successive attacks lasting all night the Zulus were beaten off, with a loss of 400 men. Naturally much was made of this in Britain to compensate for the humiliation of Isandlhwana and eleven V.C.s were awarded for the action. The value of this battle was not to be judged on grounds of sentiment and hurt pride alone, for had the Zulus captured the ford at Rorke's Drift their way would have been open to overrun the whole of Natal. As usual, Wolseley was sent from England to take the situation in hand. But before he could take command, a British army under Lord Chelmsford, who had borne the blame for the disaster at Isandlhwana, defeated 20,000 Zulus at Ulundi with a loss of fifteen British and 1500 Zulus killed, a battle which ended the power of the Zulus and of their King Cetewayo.

Eighteen months later, in 1881, came the first of the Boer Wars, when a small British force totalling some 1500 was twice badly defeated, at Laing's Nek and Majuba, by the Boers, the first white people against whom the British had measured themselves since the Crimea. The British government yielded to the Boer demand for independence and both sides settled down to wait for the next round. This came in 1899, when the Boers considered the time ripe to follow up their success of eighteen years previously with what was seen as an all-out attempt to drive the British from South Africa.

In 1882, another war started at the opposite end of Africa, in Egypt. The Egyptian Empire, under nominal Turkish rule, reached in those days from Suez south to Cape Guardafui and inland to Harrar in the southern part of Ethiopia. This great area, comprising most of the Sudan, was speedily overrun by the followers of the Mahdi, a Moslem prophet who received enthusiastic support from a population tired of Egyptian misrule. In 1884, attempts were made to bring about an orderly Egyptian evacuation of the territory, and

British troops were landed in Egypt to protect the Suez Canal from financial chaos and from the Egyptian nationalists who were in rebellion against the Khedive, the nominal viceroy of the Sultan of Turkey. To supervise the evacuation of the Sudan, the British government sent General Gordon to Khartoum. After completing his task, he was to return to England. Having reached Khartoum, Gordon refused to carry out his orders as that would have meant abandoning the people of Khartoum, and he prepared to defend Khartoum against the Mahdists. A long-drawn-out drama followed; the high-principled and disobedient Gordon continued his refusal to withdraw and a siege began which was to last for ten months.

Back in London, public opinion forced Gladstone's government to organize a relief expedition, command of which was, naturally, entrusted to Wolseley. A force of 6000 men was collected in Egypt, together with camels and other animals and boats for the transport of the force up the Nile. After delays and muddles of many kinds, the advanced guard of the British force reached Khartoum on 26 January 1885, forty-eight hours after the place had been stormed and Gordon killed. Much has naturally been made of the narrow margin of time by which the relieving force failed to save Gordon but, in fact, the Mahdists could have taken the place at any time during January, and after the New Year there had been no hope of rescue.

In the spring of 1896 the British resumed operations in the Sudan. War had broken out between Italy and Abyssinia, and the Italians appeared in danger of defeat. There was no formal understanding between Britain and Italy but it always seemed possible that they might be allies in the event of a European war. Accordingly, when Abyssinia and Italy were at war and it was likely that the Sudanese would take advantage of this to attack the Italians, the British decided that it was worthwhile to give help to the Italians by putting pressure on the Sudan. At the same time the blank spaces on the map of Africa were being rapidly filled in with the colours of conquering nations. The French, after their successes in West and Central Africa, appeared likely to expand still further until, having crossed the whole of Africa, they would occupy a broad band of territory stretching from the Atlantic to the Red Sea or the Indian Ocean. To prevent this from happening and to give relief to the Italians, it was decided once again to send an Anglo-Egyptian army to the Sudan, now under the rule of the Khalifa or Successor — successor to the Mahdi who had died six months after his capture of Khartoum. An expedition under the Sirdar or Commander-in-Chief of the Egyptian army, Sir Herbert Kitchener, was organized in Cairo and London. A total of 26,000 troops, one-third British and the rest Egyptian, was despatched up the Nile and finally met and defeated the forces, twice as numerous, of the Khalifa at Omdurman, across the river from Khartoum. The Sudanese losses numbered 15,000, the Anglo-Egyptian 500.

At this moment the prestige of the British forces stood high, but within eighteen months of Omdurman they suffered their worst

Opposite above: The headquarters of the 10th Company Royal Engineers, Suakim Field Force, 1884.

Below: Grenadier guards rest between Dervish attacks during the battle of Omdurman, 1898.

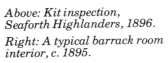

*Above: Kit inspection,
Seaforth Highlanders, 1896.*

*Right: A typical barrack room
interior, c. 1895.*

defeats since the American War of Independence. It was clear that very much was fundamentally wrong with the British army. One man who saw what the immediate future held was Wolseley, now Commander-in-Chief, but an exhausted man. He wrote on 12 September 1899, exactly a month before the Boers declared war: 'If this war comes off it will be the most serious war England has ever had.'

When the Boers declared war on 11 October 1899, their forces totalled about 90,000 men (although probably not more than half this number were in the field at any one time) against 27,000 British. Boer rifles and artillery, mostly of German origin, were superior to those of the British but, above all, the Boers were more skilled in their use.

In the field the Boers developed the concept of mounted infantry; instead of using their horses for massed cavalry charges they used them to move as quickly and as inconspicuously as possible across country. Reaching a favourable position, they would dismount, place their horses under cover and, working their way forward, prepare to engage the enemy on foot. These tactics were adopted by the British as the war went on but in its early stages British infantry was only slowly emerging from close-order drill in battle, with men standing shoulder to shoulder in full view of the enemy, firing by volleys. At the beginning of the war three Boer columns swept down into the British territories of Cape Colony and Natal and encircled three towns, henceforward to be famous because of the sieges which they underwent — Ladysmith, Mafeking and Kimberley. An immediate reaction to the disastrous start to the war by the government in London was the supersession of the British Commander-in-Chief, General Sir Redvers Buller, V.C., by Field-Marshal Lord Roberts, also a holder of the V.C.

Although the tactics of the Boers were original and highly successful, they had little idea of strategy. This was shown, in particular, in the early weeks of the war by their Commander-in-Chief, Piet Joubert. Having invaded Natal, he sat down to besiege Ladysmith instead of pressing on to the sea and Durban. Durban would have provided the land-locked republics of the Transvaal and the Orange Free State with a port through which they could have received supplies and ammunition much more easily than through neutral Lourenço Marques.

October to December 1899 was the period of Boer victories. This was followed by six months of British successes as the three principal Boer cities were taken, Bloemfontein, Pretoria and Johannesburg. However, despite the loss of both Boer capitals, the war went on for nearly two more years during which the British tried rounding up their enemy in drives right across the vast country. Bit by bit over 3000 miles of barbed-wire fences were erected, backed by some 10,000 blockhouses, garrisoned by 70,000 British and colonial troops, while the areas between the fences were swept by patrolling British and colonial columns. In all, by the end of the war in May 1902, nearly half a million British troops had been

Above: Betsy the 'international' gun being fired from the Mongol Market in Peking during the Boxer Rebellion.

Overleaf: British troops return from the South African War.

involved. Gradually the Boer units, weary and half starved, were rounded up, but until the very end they were capable of daring and successful operations, some within 100 miles of Cape Town. Three months before their final surrender, the Boers captured Lord Methuen, the senior British general in South Africa.

With the end of the war a series of inquests was held in Britain to discover what had gone wrong and what was to be done about it. Nearly every aspect of the army was investigated, from its probable role in a European war — the likelihood of which was moving from the improbable to the possible — to an all round improvement in marksmanship. The inquest took in such matters as the use of tomahawks as a cavalry weapon, the introduction for the whole army of khaki, save for ceremonial purposes, the provision of new and improved guns and rifles and the rewriting of field service regulations and training manuals. Briefly, it may be said that up to and including battalion level, the British army absorbed most of the lessons taught by the Boer War.

One thoroughgoing and completely successful reform carried out at this time was that of the standard of musketry. In 1914 the rifle-shooting of the British Expeditionary Force was first class, but in 1902 things had been very different. Lord Esher reported to the King that 'the twelve best shots fired 1210 rounds at targets, from 210 to 2600 yards distant, and had scored a total of ten hits'. It is not surprising that it was decided not to publish these results.

Unfortunately for the higher formations, there were very few useful lessons which could be learned, because most of the First World War was so very unlike the war in South Africa. Only in Palestine and Mesopotamia, the latter very much a 'side-show', were there opportunities to display experience in the handling of large bodies of men in a war of movement. Many of the leading British commanders on the Western Front had fought in South Africa, but the only one who was able to distinguish himself in the later war was Allenby, when he was sent to Palestine where South African conditions prevailed.

Although the emphasis for the future was on preparation for a possible war in Europe this did not mean that calls on the army for use overseas came to an end. Even while the Boer War was still in progress, it was necessary to send some 8000 men to China. These men joined an international force, composed of contingents from six nations, whose duty was to liberate foreigners besieged in the legation quarter of Peking, in comparative comfort, and in the Peitang cathedral, where in contrast, 3000 Christian refugees were found on the raising of the siege to be completely without food.

One of the longest-drawn-out of the 'Little Wars' continued spasmodically in British Somaliland from 1890 to 1921. It was a classic case of a daring and successful leader, Mohammed bin Abdullah, nicknamed 'the Mad Mullah', who kept British, Italian and Abyssinian Somaliland in confusion and uproar over the years by a series of well-judged raids, mostly carried out during the First World War, at a time when neither the British nor the Italians had

A typical volunteer cyclist in 1900.

any troops to spare to handle him. When peace came, the Royal Air Force was able, for the first time, to show its power to control great areas of wild country. The Dervish resistance collapsed, and Mohammed bin Abdullah died a fugitive in Abyssinia.

But from the end of the Boer War it became clearer and clearer that a huge danger, greater than any that Britain had confronted for a hundred years, was building up. From the time of Tennyson's 'Form, Riflemen, Form' in 1859, to the end of the century, many in Britain thought that an invasion of their country by the French was possible, whether or not the British navy had been defeated in battle. Accordingly, there was a clamour for increased Army Estimates, to the annoyance of the Admiralty, who begrudged army expenditure on home defence, since it held the navy perfectly capable of dealing with any threat of invasion or blockade, provided that it was strong enough. After the Boer War the situation changed. The most likely European enemy was now Germany and not France, who became, within a few years, Britain's ally.

In 1904 Lord Roberts, who had succeeded Wolseley as Commander-in-Chief of the Army in 1901, retired. The post of Commander-in-Chief was replaced by that of Chief of the Imperial General Staff. Roberts then devoted the last ten years of his life to the unsuccessful campaign for conscription in Britain. The last great reforms of the army, prior to 1914, were those carried out by R. B. Haldane, Secretary of State for War from 1906 to 1912. The most important was the creation of a territorial army of part-time soldiers which, although not highly regarded by Kitchener, became a mainstay of the British army in two world wars.

On 5 August 1914 Kitchener was appointed Secretary of State for War, in which position his overpowering personality thrust the newly appointed Chief of the Imperial General Staff, General Sir Charles Douglas, very much into the background. Within a week of the British declaration of war, the despatch of the British Expeditionary Force was under way. In the first days of the war it consisted of four infantry divisions and one cavalry division.

These events for the time being completely overshadowed the Irish question and 'the Curragh Mutiny' when, in June 1914, it appeared probable that the army would have to coerce those Ulster citizens who were determined to resist the Liberal Home Rule Bill. Rather than be placed in the position of having to use force against fellow Protestants, many Anglo-Irish officers at Curragh Camp preferred to resign their commissions. This 'mutiny' should be remembered even now, over sixty years later, as the only occasion since the reign of James II that there has ever been open disagreement between members of the officer corps of the British army and the government which they served, and that despite the fact that both before and after 1914, it is safe to say that ninety per cent of the officers of British army were more or less firm supporters of the right-wing party of the day, Tory, Conservative or Unionist. This is to be compared with the record of the French or German officer corps over this same period.

UNITED KINGDOM

History and traditions During the eighteenth and nineteenth centuries the role of the British army in world affairs was conditioned by three factors; colonial expansion, financial economy, and a determination to ensure that the army, and above all its officer corps, remained a non-political body. Although Waterloo was the last battle to be fought by a British army in western Europe for almost a century, not a year of Victoria's reign passed without a campaign in some quarter of the globe. While thus preoccupied with the Empire, the army's conception of the tactical and organizational requirements of Continental warfare fell far behind the reality. By 1854 it had become merely a collection of disparate units with little or no experience of war above regimental, or in many cases, battalion level. The regiment, with all its individual tradition and mystique, was the army; and while colonial campaigns were the chief task, this level of organization was more often than not perfectly adequate. But when the requirements of a war in the Crimea demanded the maintenance of a field army overseas, Britain's military administration dissolved into chaos. The reforms initiated as a result of this *débâcle* attempted the organization of an army which could be both an Imperial guardian, and a credible force of intervention in Europe. But the extent to which the power of tradition and insularity outweighed that of the early reforms was to be fully revealed during the Boer War.

Strength The peace establishment of the army in 1900, inclusive of British troops serving in India, was 236,172. The addition of reserves for the active army brought this strength to 343,970, and with the men of the militia, yeomanry and volunteers the total strength of British troops was approximately 684,000. To assess the war strength of Britain and her empire, the native army of India and the armies of the remaining colonies had also to be added, and this gave a strength on mobilization of 1,170,000.

System of recruiting For the purposes of recruitment and training Great Britain was divided into sixty-seven regimental districts based as far as was possible on county boundaries. Each territorial district formed an administrative brigade and it was responsible for the recruiting of two regular battalions, two militia battalions, and volunteers. The Royal Artillery drew its strength from ten recruiting areas, while the Royal Engineers recruited through the Commanding Royal Engineer in each district command.

Terms of service Service in the army was on a voluntary basis, but recruits were normally required to be between the ages of eighteen and twenty-five, to be medically fit, and to be at least five foot four inches in height. Enlistment was divided into long- and short-service terms. Long service entailing twelve

Right: Kitchener's 'boys in blue'. There were not enough khaki uniforms for the thousands of volunteers, and so an interim blue serge outfit was rapidly issued.

years active duty was confined to the Household Cavalry and certain special corps. Short service for recruits to the line cavalry, the Royal Artillery, and the Army Ordnance Corps, consisted of seven years army service followed by five years in the reserve. Enlistment in the Army Service Corps was for three years army service and nine years in the reserve. For the Foot Guards, line infantry, Medical Staff Corps, and Royal Engineers, short service presented a choice of seven years in the active army and five in the reserve, or three years and nine years respectively. For cavalry, artillery and ordnance recruits serving overseas, the terms of service were altered to eight years in the active army and four in the reserve. For Army Service Corps personnel, overseas postings could convert short service into four and eight years, while the remaining formations had the choice of eight and four years, or four and eight years. Warrant and non-commissioned officers were able to extend their service to twelve years with the colours, and soldiers of good character who had completed eleven years service could re-engage to a limit of twenty-one years. In addition, militia volunteers and regiments with 75% of their men as volunteers could be permitted to serve overseas with the regular army for not more than one year.

Officers Even by 1900 the British officer corps was still a highly selective body in which social pedigree and private income played a considerable part in an officer's career prospects. An officer passed into the army after completing a course of study and training at either the Royal Military Academy, Woolwich, for service with the artillery or engineers, or the Royal Military College, Sandhurst, for the cavalry and infantry. By comparison with Continental armies the passing-out standard at Sandhurst was low, and candidates who failed to achieve this could often receive commissions. Officers with regimental

service were trained in the higher aspects of their profession at the Staff College, Camberley.

Organization The organization of the army was designed to provide for the mobilization of all forces and for the individual mobilization of a contingent for overseas expeditions. On mobilization the field army was to consist of three army corps and four cavalry brigades, with the support of thirty-three volunteer infantry brigades and eighty-four volunteer batteries. Yeomanry brigades would be attached either to infantry brigades or the divisions of the field army. Each army corps was to consist of three infantry divisions, three cavalry squadrons, nine field batteries and supporting troops. The foreign expeditionary force consisted of 20,000 men stationed at Aldershot with their heavy equipment at Southampton.

Infantry Infantry organization was based on the principle that half of the total number of battalions would be stationed in Britain, and half overseas. The demands of unforeseen expeditionary and colonial commitments meant that it was frequently impossible to achieve this balance. The strength of home battalions was 801 officers and men, while the normal establishment of a battalion overseas was 1011. In addition to the 148 line infantry battalions there were three regiments of guards — the Grenadier, Coldstream, and Scots — and two rifle regiments — the Rifle Brigade and the King's Royal Rifle Corps.

Cavalry There were thirty-one regiments of cavalry, of which five were heavy, thirteen medium, and thirteen light. The medium cavalry included six regiments of lancers and the tendency was to increase the number of these regiments. Each regiment comprised four squadrons giving a total for the establishment of 124 squadrons. The three

regiments of Household Cavalry had a strength of twenty-four officers and 430 other ranks, while the establishment of line cavalry regiments was twenty-six officers and 696 men.

Artillery The Royal Artillery was divided into two regiments, one of horse and field artillery, the other of garrison and mountain artillery. The establishment provided for twenty-four horse artillery batteries (eleven in India), 103 field artillery batteries (forty-two in India), 110 garrison batteries, and ten mountain batteries.

Engineers The sixty-two and a half companies of Royal Engineers included bridging, telegraph, balloon, mining, and railway troops. In war, four field companies of engineers were assigned to each army corps.

Militia The militia was designed to provide a body of trained troops for the defence of Great Britain, and for the purpose of reinforcing the units of the regular army on mobilization. Service was for six years and included six months preliminary training followed by annual courses of from twenty-seven to fifty-six days.

Volunteers The volunteers, who included the yeomanry and whose number stood at approximately 250,000, could be called out for military service as units or as individuals. The annual training requirement was eight days service.

The Cardwell system had failed to resolve Britain's conflicting manpower needs and her army remained inadequate for Continental or major colonial wars. But the British Army of 1900 had suffered its Black Week (10-17 December 1899) and a movement in favour of change and reorganization was gradually to gather momentum.

1st Life Guards on their departure for France in autumn 1914.

2 INDIA

British supremacy in India is generally held to have dated from Clive's victory at Plassey in 1757, when one thousand British troops and two thousand of their Indian allies defeated a force seventeen times as great, composed of Indians who were allies of France.

Although there was much hard fighting in the war after 1757, this date maintained its importance in the minds of men. One of the myriad rumours, which continually swept across India, held that British rule would last exactly one hundred years, and as the year 1857 drew nearer the belief represented by the rumour grew in strength. There existed no hard basis for fears felt at the time, but it was soon seen that there was much dry tinder lying about, and all it needed was a spark.

The spark, when it came, was the issue of the famous greased cartridges which, according to regulations, had to be bitten open before being placed in the muzzle of the rifle. Indian soldiers suspected that the grease might include beef or pork fat, the taste of which would mean religious defilement for Hindu or Moslem alike. These protests were strengthened by a growing belief that the British were carrying out a gradual drive to convert the people of India to Christianity. Official enquiries revealed later that no one knew for certain what fat was used for the cartridges; no one had bothered to find out. No one had drawn attention to the capital importance of the point, or insisted that the grease used should not contain animal fat. Similarly, only a few units with more intelligent officers had discovered that the cartridges could, in fact, be loaded without being bitten at all.

This slackness by the British authorities was typical of a decline in the quality of the men who commanded the British and Indian troops protecting the borders of India and who were the ultimate sanction for the maintenance of order, both external and internal. How far things had deteriorated was shown when the Mutiny was over and it was established that, of the commanding officers of seventy-three units which had taken part in the Mutiny and who had survived, only four were fit for re-appointment to command.

It must be remembered that at this time India was, in theory at least, a collection of Indian territories administered by the Honourable East India Company in London, for the ineffectual Mogul Emperor in Delhi. According to this theory the Company was acting only as the agent of the Delhi government, but it became plain as the years passed that it was the supreme authority in the country, imposing taxes and maintaining its own army and navy. Of the army, some units were composed of European troops and some of Indian. In addition, the British government loaned units of the British army, whose pay was then a charge upon the Indian budget.

In 1857, at the commencement of the Mutiny, there were altogether in India 36,000 white troops and 257,000 Indian. Of the white troops, two regiments of cavalry were Queen's troops and three Company's, and of twenty-nine regiments of infantry, twenty were Queen's troops and nine Company's, while all the artillery was the Company's. So very thin on the ground were troops of any sort that there was only one regiment between Calcutta and Dinapur, a distance of 400 miles. This was, in part, because wars in Russia, Persia and China had drawn off a substantial proportion of the units of the British army. In India, people were quick to draw the conclusion that the British hold on the country was loosening.

At this time the British and Indian forces in India were organized in three commands; the Bengal army, which was the senior and whose commander was also Commander-in-Chief in India, the Bombay army and the Madras army. The Mutiny was almost entirely the work of units of the Bengal army; of 130,000 men in this command about 70,000 joined the rebels, 30,000 either deserted the colours or were disarmed by the British, while 30,000 remained loyal, as did almost all the troops in the two armies of Bombay and Madras, totalling about 150,000. Accordingly, as Dr S. N. Sen points out in *1857*, the first official Indian account of the Mutiny, the war which followed was not a struggle of British against Indians, but of British and their Indian allies against other Indians. As far as the Indians were concerned, it was very largely a matter for soldiers, except for a few native rulers who sought what advantage they could. The ordinary Indian civilian, whether merchant or cultivator, high or low caste, generally kept out of the way in much the same manner as ordinary Englishmen did during the Wars of the Roses.

Recovering from their surprise, the British and their allies fought their way back into control of all India and sealed this with the annexation of the Honourable East India Company's territories to the Crown. This also meant the demise of the Company's army and the urgent necessity for the creation of a new one. There was, however, no attempt to make a clean sweep and a fresh beginning, partly perhaps because of innate conservatism, partly because it was considered that much of value had, in fact, survived. But what had not survived and what seems never to have been entirely restored was the old feeling of confidence and trust which had existed between British and Indian. Both remembered all too well the atrocities, real and alleged, committed by the two sides. The British, who had only 6500 administrators with 70,000 British and 140,000 Indian soldiers with which to control and defend a country with a population of 300 million, never shook themselves completely free from the feeling that it could happen again.

As a first move in the reorganization of the forces in India, the European infantry units of the Company's forces were transferred to the regular British army. A new recruiting policy for Indian units was also introduced at this time; recruiting in Bengal was severely cut back, as was recruiting in the Madras presidency. In future, it was intended to concentrate on recruiting from the so-called 'martial races' in northern India, a policy which was continued up till the Second World War, despite a great deal of running criticism by those who believed that the race of an Indian soldier did not affect his fighting capabilities. Controversy over this was to last for almost all the remaining years of British rule, but it came as near to being

Above: Soldiers standing outside the shell-battered Dewan Khas Palace in Lucknow following Sir Colin Campbell's relief of the residency, November 1857.

*Below: No. 4 (Hazara)
Mountain Battery on the
Punjab frontier, 1897.*

settled as possible by the belated discovery that Indian troops, well trained and well led, fought well no matter whence they came. Meanwhile, the British made a good deal of unnecessary trouble for themselves by their lack of interest in recruiting from the south. For, in the south, there was much less concern over matters of caste, which were a constant preoccupation with the 'martial races' of the north.

The post-Mutiny scheme of reorganization was completed by 1863, a year marked by the mutiny of all eight regiments of Bengal cavalry, but this was the last flicker of the Great Mutiny, rather than the start of fresh trouble. It was now possible to plan the role of the British and Indian forces, whose strengths were re-established in the old ratio of one-third British to two-thirds Indian in the future defence of the country. In the first place, it was necessary to defend the borders of India against foreign aggression (which in most men's minds meant Russia), until reinforcements could be brought from the rest of the Empire. In the meantime the Indian forces were without artillery and equipped with semi-obsolete weapons, partly for reasons of economy. For the same reason, no considerable reserve for the Indian army was created.

The main area for concentration of the armies in India was the north-west frontier, the geography of which has been thus described by Philip Mason, the historian of the Indian army and the Indian Civil Service: 'Terrible country, harsh, fierce and jagged, rocky peak, serrated edge, dry, icy upland, stony breathless valley, that pens up the heat, a marksman behind every rock, a war of sniping and ambush and long marches at night, occasionally the rush of yelling fanatics sworn to die for the faith of Mohammed.' This was to be life on the north-west frontier for the next eighty years and because the Indian and British armies could cope successfully with it, the millions inside the frontier were able to live in peace.

But there was work for the Indian army outside India as well. Indian troops, with their elephants, took part in the Abyssinian campaign of 1867 and it became obvious that the Indian army could be used overseas in time of emergency just as the old Company's army had been, fighting in Java, in the Philippines and in Malaya. It was established that, whereas the Indian government paid the cost of British and Indian troops inside India, any additional cost of operations serving outside India was to be paid by the Imperial government in London.

From the point of view of organization there now followed a long period of development lasting until 1914; what did not develop was the status of the Indian officer. Even as late as 1914 an Indian officer at more than platoon level was a great rarity; but successive emergencies pried loose the grip of custom so that, at the beginning of the Second World War, there were Indian captains and majors, and at the end of that war, on the eve of independence, there were brigadiers and colonels.

All through these years, however, the type of the Indian other rank remained almost entirely unchanged; he usually came from a family in which two, three, or more generations had served in the army and probably in the same regiment. To quote Philip Mason again:

It was a mercenary army. It was not from patriotic motives that the sepoy enlisted, but because the army — as a rule — was his hereditary profession, because it brought him an adequate livelihood together with social position, consequence and honour. The sepoy was a middle-class man, much more akin to D'Artagnan and Porthos than to Thomas Atkins. He went on leave with a man to carry his bundle; even on a campaign there were five followers to one fighting man. He was proud of himself and of his profession. He had a fierce pride in the colours of his regiment, which, if he was a Hindu, he worshipped yearly with the same rites the peasant used before his plough, the smith before his tools.

If the Indian soldier was excellent material, his British officer too was of quality much above average. In the first place, competition for a commission in the Indian army was keen; it was a service in which private means were hardly necessary, and frequent spells of active service were, in themselves, a very great attraction compared to barrack life back in England.

Between 1863, when the Indian army was just emerging from a state of convalescence after the Mutiny, and 1913 there were no fewer than forty-five expeditions undertaken by British or Indian forces against tribes whose existence was based upon raiding into the peaceful and more prosperous valleys of the north-west frontier. These expeditions ranged in size from a few hundred men to the greatest of them all, the Tirah campaign of 1897, in which the British and Indian forces totalled four divisions. The origin of the tribesmen's decision to attack at this time appears to have been news of the victory secured by the Turks over the Greeks in the brief war of the same year; this, it was claimed, clearly indicated a great Moslem resurgence and the tribesmen were not to be outdone by their Turkish co-religionists.

But, in addition to these operations, between 1878 and 1881 a full-scale war was conducted against Afghanistan. This had been occasioned by the perennial British fear that Russian influence had so penetrated Afghanistan that a Russian invasion of India would be possible at any time. Early British successes, notably by the force under the command of Roberts, brought about a peace which, however, was soon broken by the murder of the British envoy and his staff in Kabul. Swift reaction, in which Roberts again distinguished himself, and the abdication of the Amir of Afghanistan, left the British, superficially at least, rulers of the whole country. But the British forces were far too small for the task and a series of Afghan counter-attacks, uncoordinated yet formidable, caused the British and Indian garrison at Kabul, greatly outnumbered, to fall back northwards to the fort of Sherpur. Here, two days before Christmas 1879, they were attacked by a force of 100,000 Afghans; six hours fighting followed, at the end of which the entire enemy force disappeared and Kabul was retaken.

British officers of 11th King Edward's Own Lancers in full dress, 1907.

The next move by the British and Indian governments was an attempt to install a new Amir on the Afghan throne resulting in a civil war. During the fighting, a mixed British and Indian brigade was nearly wiped out at Maiwand and Kandahar was threatened. Roberts was sent to the rescue and his dramatic, successful march from Kabul to Kandahar secured his fame and later his title of Earl Roberts of Kandahar. In 1885, he was appointed Commander-in-Chief in India. He began by reorganizing or, in many cases organizing from the beginning, most aspects of the army transport, supply and training, the chief aim of his drive being to fit the Indian army to fight a European enemy. In pursuance of this aim he led off with a blast at the three presidency headquarters, Madras, Bombay and Bengal, denouncing those working there as 'idle, mercenary drones'. The presidencies, however, survived until 1895. Roberts began his reforms with the decision that, rather than base the power of the army upon fixed fortifications, he would prepare for a campaign of movement by building roads and railways.

The Russian menace was a permanent fixture from generation to generation in India, from pre-Kipling to post-Kitchener, despite the fact that experts persisted in saying that an invasion of India through Afghanistan was an impossibility. This was backed up by

Below: Garrison artillery with heavy (40-pounders) battery in elephant draught, 1897.

the investigations of a committee which came to the conclusion that a Russian force strong enough to overcome the difficulties of keeping supply routes open through Afghanistan and to maintain a force big enough to defeat the British and Indian troops when it emerged from Afghanistan into India, would require over four million camels.

Nevertheless, Kitchener, who was appointed Commander-in-Chief in India in 1902 and served in that post for seven years, made his priority a reorganization of the disposition of his forces to meet a Russian threat and to cover the two routes that led from Afghanistan into India. To the north was Peshawar and the Khyber, to the south was the road from Quetta to Kandahar. Behind these two gateways, lines of communication ran back from Peshawar to Calcutta and from Quetta to Mhow and Bombay. Nine divisions in all were held ready to march, five by the northern route and four by the southern.

In making these dispositions Kitchener found himself confronted by the old divided command which had officially been abolished in 1895 but which, in fact, still existed. Kitchener succeeded finally in ridding India of this system and this was probably the greatest service which he rendered during his term of office. In addition, within two years of arriving in India he succeeded in bringing about the resignation of the Viceroy, Lord Curzon, one of the most imposing of the men whose lives spanned the gap between the later years of Queen Victoria and the end of the First World War. But

Kitchener was just as imposing. It was the meeting of the irresistible force and the immovable body, and Kitchener, the irresistible force, won.

The matter of the dispute was the authority of the Military Member of the Viceroy's Council. Kitchener, as Commander-in-Chief, insisted that the Military Member should be subordinate to his authority. The Viceroy, on the other hand, insisted that the Military Member should be senior to the Commander-in-Chief, in the same way that the Secretary of State for War in London had authority over the Chief of the Imperial General Staff. Curzon appealed to the Prime Minister, Arthur Balfour, saying that the British government should choose between him and Kitchener. It did so, choosing Kitchener and Curzon resigned, leaving Kitchener regretting that he had not been able to challenge the Viceroy to a duel. Kitchener was now supreme and remained so until his term of office expired in 1909. He left behind something of an administrative desert. He had a ferocious hatred of paperwork, so great that he would avoid, whenever possible, important meetings at which he knew that a shorthand writer would be present.

This attitude of the Commander-in-Chief had its effect on his staff: they either neglected their own paperwork or performed it badly. This influence at G.H.Q. in India persisted after Kitchener returned to Europe and its tragic result was the disgraceful failure of the campaign in Mesopotamia when the medical and supply services collapsed and great and unnecessary suffering followed.

INDIA

History and traditions Until April 1895 the Indian army was divided into three distinct army systems based on the presidencies of Bengal, Madras and Bombay. These armies were steadily increased during the first half of the nineteenth century under the stimulus of border wars and annexations. The Madras army was recruited from the presidency and its native states and consisted mainly of Mohammedans, Brahmans, and Mahrattas. The Bengal army was drawn from Hindustan and comprised Hindus, Mohammedans, and an element of Gurkhas recruited in Nepal. The Bombay army consisted chiefly of Mahrattas, Mohammedans and Hindus recruited in the presidency. Before the reorganization of 1860 the British officers for all three native armies were supplied from the East India Company's military college at Addiscombe, or by direct appointment.

Strength The native army had a strength of 148,000 regular troops, with reserves of 20,000, and a volunteer force of 30,000.

Terms of service There was no conscription while the native army remained under British rule and every recruit was a volunteer. A soldier qualified for a pension after twenty-one years service.

Organization On the abolition of the presidency armies, the native forces were divided into four army corps — the Punjab, Madras, Bombay and Bengal. Their establishment totalled forty cavalry regiments, 133 infantry battalions, thirteen artillery batteries and twenty-two companies of sappers and miners. Internally, companies and, to some degree, regiments were organized as far as possible to place men of the same class — by virtue of religion, caste or race — together.

For much of the second half of the nineteenth century, the standards of training and leadership in the Indian army were considerably higher than those displayed by the British army. Moreover, the Indian army was on a permanent war footing, and it provided Britain with a large professional force, whenever and wherever it was needed. During World War I, India's contribution in manpower (1,300,000 by 1918) was greater than that of any other part of the Empire save that of Britain itself.

The Khan of Lalpura with followers during the Second Afghan War, 1878-80.

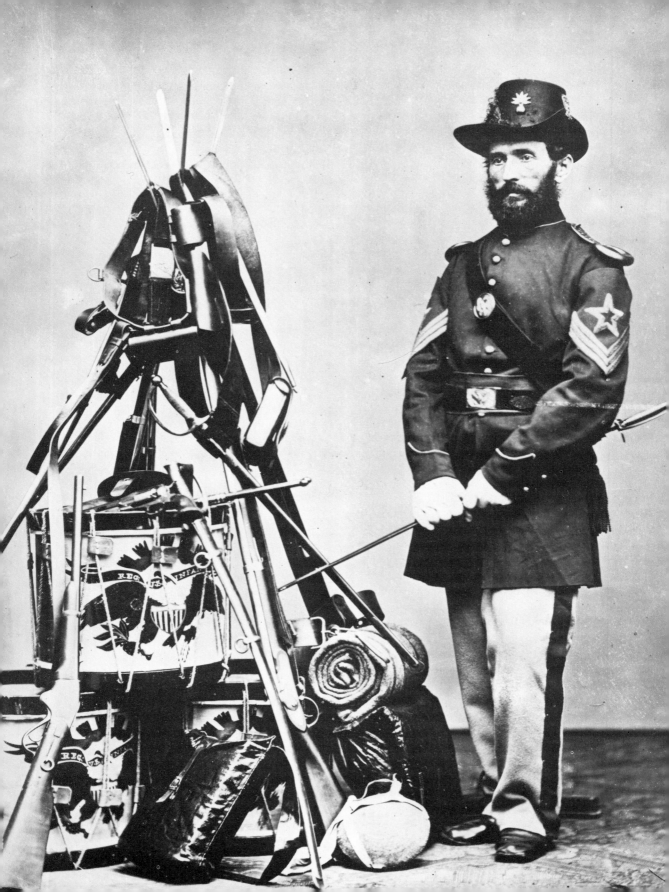

3 UNITED STATES

Between the end of the war with Britain in 1815 and the outbreak of war with Mexico in 1846, the United States was at peace. The army, usually about 9000 strong, was for the most part stationed in small posts, sited to give the best possible protection for settlers against the Indian marauders, who were fighting a losing battle against white men and the long lines of their wagons rolling westward.

In 1836 some of these settlers, established in the Mexican district of Texas, had risen against the Mexican government and proclaimed Texas an independent republic. Ten years later the independent republic was taken over by the United States and, with it, a boundary dispute between Mexico and Texas concerning the ownership of the land between the River Nueces and the Rio Grande. War was declared on Mexico by the United States on 13 May 1846 and a beginning was made in expanding the army, which eventually reached a strength of nearly 80,000 volunteers.

The main body of the United States force was concentrated under General Zachary Taylor at the mouth of the Rio Grande and began a very deliberate advance into Mexican territory. Meanwhile, a small force of 1700 men, styled 'the Army of the West', left Fort Leavenworth in Kansas under Colonel Stephen Kearny on 29 June with orders to take the port of San Diego on the Pacific coast 1400 miles away. After one small engagement in which eighteen men were killed, Kearny reached San Diego on 12 December, to find the United States navy in possession. Another long range penetration similar to that of Kearny was carried out by the 1st Missouri Mounted Volunteers under Colonel Doniphan. Doniphan, having accompanied Kearny as far as the Mexican border, then turned south-east and, after a sweep of 3500 miles, linked up with a force under General Wool which had covered 900 miles from San Antonio to join Taylor's main force. Taylor's own progress had been slow and President Polk, dissatisfied, had ordered him to stand fast and to detach 7000 men from his command who were sent to Matamoros at the mouth of the Rio Grande to form part of the first amphibious force in United States history. Under the command of General Scott these troops were sent by sea to Vera Cruz, where they landed on 29 March 1847, and began an advance up country towards Mexico City, the Mexican capital. Meanwhile Taylor had disobeyed his orders to remain on the defensive and had fought and won the battle of Buena Vista on 27 February. His force was outnumbered by about three to

Opposite: One of a series of photographs taken by the Quartermaster Depot in Philadelphia, 1861-2, showing types of United States army uniforms. This photograph shows an ordnance sergeant.

one, but the exhausted and poorly trained Mexican troops were repulsed during a two-day fight; Mexican casualties numbering about 1500 and those of the Americans about 750. After this Santa Anna, the defeated Mexican general, fell back on Mexico City.

However, the war was decided by Scott and his troops, who slogged their way up from the sea. They broke into the interior of Mexico at Cerro Gordo on 18 April after a reconnaissance by two captains of the engineers, Robert E. Lee and George B. McClellan who, fifteen years later, were to find themselves opposing commanders at the critical battle of Antietam. Lee and McClellan were just two of the junior officers who distinguished themselves in this war and rose to the highest ranks in the Civil War of 1861-5. Others included Ulysses S. Grant, who became General-in-Chief of the Northern forces in March 1864 and led them to final victory; Jefferson Davis, who was elected Confederate President; George Meade, who commanded the Union forces at Gettysburg; Joseph C. Johnston who commanded the Confederate Department of the West; and Stonewall Jackson. After a further short advance, Scott was obliged to halt for nearly three months, awaiting reinforcements from home to replace troops whose short term of enlistment had expired. Finally the advance was resumed in August and Mexico City taken on 14 September.

Under the terms of the Treaty of Guadalupe Hidalgo, which ended the war, Mexico ceded some 500,000 square miles of territory (about one-sixth of the total area of the continental United States), including what are now the states of California, New Mexico, Arizona, Nevada, Utah and parts of Colorado, Idaho and Wyoming. All the newly-won land became slave territory, except for California. These gains for slavery represented a great success for the pro-slavery South and it was for this reason that the war against Mexico had been undertaken in the first place. Nevertheless, the 'hawkish' Southern states were disappointed, for they wanted the annexation of all of Mexico and fought hard to prevent the ratification of the treaty by the Senate.

As for the army, reduced by demobilization to between nine and ten thousand men, it returned to the work of protecting the settlers against the Indians. There was, however, only one important operation between the army and the Indians during the period between the end of the Mexican war and the outbreak of the Civil War. This began when the Sioux and the Cheyenne Indians raided the California trail near Fort Laramie, in Wyoming, wiping out an army patrol on 19 August 1854. In the following year, the United States government organized a punitive expedition and 1200 cavalrymen were despatched in search of the culprits, who were discovered at Ash Hollow in Nebraska and almost entirely wiped out; 136 men being killed.

When the Civil War began on 12 April 1861, the United States army numbered 15,000 men, most of them still stationed in Indian country. The war lasted almost exactly four years and during that time the Northern, Federal or Union forces were expanded by

Below: Union belt buckle.
Opposite: Confederate belt
buckle.

voluntary enlistment and conscription ('the draft') to a strength of more than two million, or about 45% of the total male population of military age. Southern, Confederate or rebel states recruited about half that number, representing 90% of men of military age, both volunteers and conscripts. When the war was at its height, there were some three million men under arms, about one-tenth of the total population of men, women and children of the North and South combined. This proportion is almost exactly the same as that of men and women called up in the United States during the Second World War. In the course of the war, half a million men were killed or died from disease (as was usually the case in the wars of those days, deaths from disease outnumbered those in battle). The proportion of deaths to total population was much the same as that suffered by the United Kingdom in the First World War, leaving aside Dominion, Colonial and Indian losses.

By the end of the Civil War there had developed armies that were the model for those who were to go to war in 1914. They differed only in the lack of the internal combustion engine, and consequently of motor transport and aircraft (apart from balloons). Above all, development of the railway and the telegraph system made it possible to concentrate, move, and supply great armies for the first time. As the war went on the whole picture of the battlefield changed. The introduction of breech-loading rifles meant that it was no longer necessary to stand up to load and the sight of men standing shoulder to shoulder firing in volleys disappeared. Men were able to load and fire lying down from behind any cover that they could find, and, when possible, extemporizing by digging what became known to the American army in successive wars as 'rifle-pits', 'trenches' and 'foxholes'.

Even the dress of the soldiers reflected the change coming over land warfare in the twentieth century. The exuberant uniforms of

the first volunteers on both sides soon gave way to the classic blue and grey which were to become famous, although the grey of the Southern forces was replaced, for other ranks at least, with dyed wool of a vague, pale brown shade, known as 'butternut', produced by a mixture of crushed walnut shells, because of a lack of other dyes.

At the beginning of the war, Lincoln's government in Washington decided to increase the regular army by new enlistment to a total of 42,000, whose duty it would be to protect Union-held territory against Indian raiders and marauders. The Southern rebellion would be put down by volunteer forces to be raised under the auspices of the governments of the states. It was also decided by the Confederates that their constituent states should do the same, volunteers being enrolled for one year. In the North, it was expected that the emergency would be a short one and the first enlistments were only for ninety days. The volunteers took this time limit very literally; even troops fighting in the first important battle of the war, at Bull Run, left the battlefield when their ninety-day enlistment was at an end and started for home. This situation was, of course, impossible. The period of enlistment was raised to three years and, at the same time, a cash bounty was offered to recruits. An important mistake made in organizing the new armies was the decision to form newly trained men into fresh units, instead of using them to take the place of casualties in the old units. As a result, the latter wasted away until they became so weak as to be useless and had to be broken up. Many officers of the units disbanded in this way were discharged as well, although they had irreproachable records of up to three years service. This was partly because state governors wished to exercise political patronage by providing new — and inexperienced — men.

The bounty seriously handicapped recruiting for the regular

army, which could offer no such inducement. Officers serving in the regular army were also seriously discriminated against. Officers for the new volunteer units, up to the rank of brigadier general, were selected by the governors of the states and the obvious place in which to look for potential officer material was amongst the many younger retired officers. For it had become usual for subaltern and field officers, bored by peace-time service after the excitements of the war with Mexico, to retire and go into business or one of the professions in the boom days before the Civil War. Thus famous

Confederate camp at Warrington navy yard, Florida 1861.

leaders on both sides, including Grant, Sherman, Jackson and McClellan, found themselves in great demand and recipients of extremely accelerated promotion. McClellan, thirty-four years old at the beginning of the war, rose within seven months from captain on the retired list to Commander-in-Chief of the Army, a post which he held for five months. He was then suspended in April 1862, re-appointed in August of the same year and finally replaced five months later. This was an extreme case but, while retired officers were being promoted, their contemporaries who had remained in the regular army were fated in many cases to go through the war with hardly a step in rank. On the other hand, Colonel Boatner in his encyclopaedic *Civil War Dictionary,* writes: 'The 102 West Pointers who came back into service from civil life during the war were in a position to "shop around" for an assignment with volunteer units; 51 of these became generals.'

The Confederate states, on the other hand, based their officer corps in the first place on men from the regular army who had resigned their commissions to go with their states when these seceded. Official records show that, out of a total of 1080 officers in the regular army at the beginning of the war, 313 resigned to join the Confederate states. Of these, the man with by far the greatest reputation within the army was Colonel Robert E. Lee who, on the recommendation of Scott, then General-in-Chief of the Army, was offered command of the Union forces by Lincoln. Lee refused the offer and left the service to take command of the forces of his native state, Virginia, then on the point of secession. After having served as military adviser to the Confederate President he was appointed, on 1 June 1862, to the Confederacy's senior command, that of the Army of Northern Virginia, whose role in the war was to threaten directly the Northern capital of Washington and to defend the Southern capital of Richmond, Virginia.

While a third of the officer corps followed their states into secession, of the 15,000 other ranks only twenty-six were known to 'have deserted to the Confederacy at the outbreak of war'. An odd feature of the career structure of the Federal officer corps was the fact that, despite nearly two million men being under arms, it was not until March 1864, when Grant was promoted, that there was any officer above the rank of major-general.

The war began in Charleston Harbour, where the troops of the state of South Carolina opened fire on a small garrison (87 officers and men) of Federal troops in Fort Sumter, which was obliged to surrender after only a brief resistance. The war spread through the Southern states and a number of scattered small engagements took place, but the first crisis of the war built itself up just outside Washington. By July 1861 the North had 190,000 troops under arms, while the South had about half that number. Of these forces, 50,000 Northerners had been concentrated for the defence of Washington and 20,000 Confederates faced them at Manassas. The odds seemed very much against the latter and although the Federal troops were mostly only three-month volunteers it was decided that

Confederate picket near Charleston, South Carolina, in 1861.

they should attack. The advance on Manassas was a shambles; it took two and a half days to march twenty miles. When the Confederates counter-attacked, however, the retreat of the Northern troops was very much faster, even along roads cluttered by long lines of carriages of the wealthy and curious from Washington who had been anxious not to miss what, many believed, would be the only battle of the war.

The Confederates were no better trained than the Northerners, and although they advanced with great good heart they were soon completely disorganized and the threat to Washington faded for the time being. The performance of both sides gave rise to hopes that the war might not be fought seriously but, after a winter spent by North and South trying to create disciplined and efficient forces, the first big battle of the spring, fought at Shiloh in Tennessee on 6 and 7 April, completely dashed these hopes.

C. F. Atkinson writes: 'The battle of Shiloh was a savage scuffle between two half-disciplined hosts, contested with a fury rare even in this war.' Moltke's view that the American Civil War could be dismissed as a matter of two armed mobs chasing each other round the countryside ('a view for which' comments Hugh Brogan 'there is somewhat more to be said than is usually allowed') was founded on this kind of battle, but the fact remains that both sides lost a quarter of their strength, a proportion of losses which horrified people at home and which presaged a war in which the only end could be 'unconditional surrender'. The result of the battle of Shiloh was a narrow win for the North, whose commander, Ulysses S. Grant, was now on his way to the supreme command and the presidency of the United States; with him on his way up the ladder of promotion was to travel one of his divisional commanders at Shiloh, William T. Sherman. The Confederate Commander-in-Chief, General Albert Sidney Johnston, was mortally wounded during the battle.

The Shiloh campaign was the first of a series of operations which, in the ensuing eighteen months, cut the Confederacy in half from north to south along the line of the Mississippi. It was, however, the fighting over the 110-mile stretch of Virginia between Washington and Richmond which caught the headlines during the war in the first place, and held the history books in the years to come. Later writings have made it clear that the two Northern offensives, east and west of the Appalachians, supported each other mutually and effectively until the war's end.

Two days before the battle of Shiloh, the main Northern force, the 150,000-strong Army of the Potomac, now commanded by McClellan, began an imaginative operation which was designed to finish the war within a few weeks. Embarking twelve divisions in a fleet of transports covered by the United States navy, he moved them down the coast and landed them to the south-east of Richmond, on the peninsula between the York and James Rivers. But there was a complete failure to exploit the advantages of the new position and the Federal advance to the north-west ground to a halt six miles from Richmond. In this emergency, with Joseph E. Johnston, the Confederate commander, seriously wounded and his capital in danger, Jefferson Davis appointed his military adviser Robert E. Lee to command the Army of Northern Virginia on 1 June 1862.

Heavy fighting followed; the North could not make the extra effort needed to take Richmond, the South could not destroy the Northern army which, thwarted, withdrew once more to its original position between Washington and Richmond. An important reason for McClellan's failure in this operation had been the progress of Stonewall Jackson's famous campaign in the Shenandoah Valley which caused Lincoln to insist that troops, which had been intended for McClellan in the peninsula, should be held back for the protection of Washington.

Jackson, with 4200 infantry moving at such a rate that they nicknamed themselves 'the Foot Cavalry', stormed up and down the valley for three months, on one occasion marching sixty miles in two days under a blazing August sun with many men barefoot. They not only swept the valley clear of Union troops but threatened to emerge through one of the gaps in the Blue Ridge Mountains on the flank of the Union forces which were defending Washington and threatening Richmond. Lee was then able to plan and carry out the first of two great blows against the North which, if successful, might have brought the war to an end. For, as has frequently been pointed out, to achieve victory the North had to occupy Richmond and the whole of the Confederacy while the South needed only to convince the

North that the cost of forcing the seceding states back into the Union was too great.

By August Lee was ready for the first of the two great invasions of the North. While it was just possible that either of these invasions might have resulted in the capture of Washington, nobody anticipated an outcome such as the capture of New York or the occupation of the great areas of Northern territory. It was, however, believed by the Southerners that, were they to win a series of striking victories, the North would be convinced that the defeat of the South would require much more effort than would be worthwhile, so that it would be best to agree to the independence of the South. This view reflects a degree of contempt which Southerners felt for Northerners, who were seen as committed to making money and enjoying the trappings of civilization. Indeed, it was a view which had been taken, and was to be taken, of the American people by their enemies in most crises of their history. The British during the Revolutionary War and the War of 1812 thought in this way, as did the Germans in

Below left: Confederate prisoners taken during the battle of Gettysburg, July 1863.

Below right: Union infantry at Fredricksburg in May 1863.

the First World War and the Germans and the Japanese in the Second World War.

The first of the great Confederate invasions of the North ended at Antietam in Maryland on 17 September 1862. The battle, however, was drawn; and this meant that the Southern troops could not hold their advanced position on Northern territory and were compelled to withdraw behind the Potomac.

In the summer of 1863, after two brilliantly successful defensive battles at Fredricksburg and Chancellorsville in Virginia, Lee was ready for another invasion of the North, despite the loss of his most able lieutenant, Stonewall Jackson, who had been accidentally wounded by his own men, dying within a few days. Now Lee went further into Northern territory than he had ever gone before, or was ever to do again, and his capture of Gettysburg was to make the little Pennsylvania town immortal. It had been selected as the objective for the first part of the Southern advance because of the reported presence in the town of 40,000 pairs of new boots, a

priceless treasure for the South, cut off as they were by a stringent Northern blockade from overseas sources of supply. There had been a similar shortage of small arms at the beginning of 1862, when troops were armed with shotguns and smooth-bore muskets, but the succession of Southern victories had provided as spoils some 100,000 modern rifles so that, for a few months, this particular problem was solved.

By 4 July 1863, after three days hard fighting, the North took Gettysburg and on the same day another important victory was gained by the Northern forces at Vicksburg on the Mississippi. For eighteen months they had been fighting their way up the Mississippi from its mouth and down the river from the north, to take possession of this vital line of communication and to cut the Confederacy in two. Finally Vicksburg was taken and Grant was able to signal to Washington 'The Father of Waters flows unvexed to the Sea'. The war had travelled another great stage towards its end and within eight months Grant became General-in-Chief.

Gettysburg and Vicksburg together with the Northern blockade decided the war, although fighting went on for twenty months longer. Within nine days of the two victories a mob of 50,000 was rioting in New York, killing, looting and setting fire to public buildings in protest against the introduction of conscription, and order was only re-established after more than a thousand people had been killed or wounded.

As the war continued and the position of the South grew worse, desertions from the Southern forces greatly increased. With all the fighting now in progress on Southern soil, it was easy for a man to slip away from his unit and find friendly shelter. Even as early as the Antietam campaign, it was reported that Lee's stragglers totalled a third to a half of his entire force. Six months before the end of the war, according to the *Richmond Enquirer,* President Jefferson Davis 'emphatically announced that two-thirds of the army were absent from the ranks'. On the Northern side, desertions totalled about 268,000, largely due to the practice of 'bounty jumping', by which men would enlist, draw their bounty, desert, re-enlist, collect another bounty and so on, until they were caught or the war ended.

*   *   *   *

The story of the Civil War after Gettysburg and Vicksburg was that of a long retreat, or rather of two long retreats by the Confederates, which lasted until the end of the war in the spring of 1865.

In the east, the Army of the Potomac began another drive on Richmond in the spring of 1864, slogging through the area known as 'the Wilderness' in a Somme-like campaign. In the west, Sherman, commanding the military division of the Mississippi, began another campaign on 7 May, in which his army fought its way across country until it reached Atlanta on 1 September 1864, and started its famous march through Georgia. This was achieved on 21 December and, after a pause to re-group, Sherman turned northward,

iam J. Jackson
Serg_t May 12_th N.Y. Vol.
d at Stoneman's Switch
near Fredericksburg V_a
Jan 27_th /63

141

VOLUNTEER ARMIES

Right: Second-Lieutenant George Armstrong Custer meets his former class-mate from West Point, Second-Lieutenant Washington, C.S.A., who had just been taken prisoner, 31 May 1862.

Below: General Ulysses Simpson Grant, United States Army, Autumn 1863 (left), and General Robert E. Lee, Confederate States army in April 1865 (right).

pursuing the remnants of the Army of Tennessee commanded by Joseph E. Johnston, as it made its way northward to join Lee.

But, finally driven from Richmond on 2 April, Lee was pursued westward and surrounded at Appomattox with his army of 26,000 men. Here, the immaculately dressed Lee surrendered to a tousled and dishevelled Grant. The respective states of their uniforms on this occasion was ever after a source of embarassment and regret to Grant, who recalled that the last time they had met, during the Mexican War, Lee, then his superior officer, had reproved him for his slovenly appearance. Seventeen days after Appomattox, Johnston was caught and compelled, in his turn, to surrender.

The war was now virtually over. After Lee's surrender there were still 150,000 Confederate troops in the field, but by the beginning of June these had all faded away, the last formed units surrendering at Galveston, Texas on 2 June, after Jefferson Davis had been captured on 10 May on his way to Texas to continue the struggle.

There were, however, Southerners who could not face the prospect of returning beaten to their homes and who sought a new life abroad, mostly in Latin America, the favourite country of exile being Mexico. Here they had high hopes that their talents would be employed in the civil war then in progress between the forces of Emperor Maximilian (who was installed on the Mexican throne and then abandoned by Napoleon III) and the Republicans under Benito Juarez.

The man who came nearest to achieving this aim was Brigadier General Joseph O. Shelby, commander of the Iron Brigade of the Confederate army, who led the remnants of his force into Mexico in an attempt to continue his military career. He sold his heavy weapons to the Republicans and then continued southward to place himself and his men at the disposal of the Emperor. Maximilian, however, refused his offer for fear of offending the United States. Nevertheless, a few former Confederate officers were able to soldier on and three even became generals in the Egyptian army.

Within a few months of Appomattox both the great American armies had disappeared, leaving the United States regular army to fight the Indians in a series of campaigns which lasted for two decades.

Thanks to television and the cinema, the names of men and places concerned in small skirmishes in these frontier wars are, in many cases, better known that those of the leaders and battles of the tremendous war which had just ended. The Sioux wars; the Cheyenne and Arapahoe; the Apache wars; and the Indian leaders; Black Hawk, Crazy Horse, Sitting Bull and Geronimo who, during the nineteenth century, carried on the vain struggle, are well known. Fort Laramie, Wounded Knee and Little Big Horn are household names in many parts of the globe, while, outside the United States, Shiloh, Manassas, Vicksburg and the rest are familiar only to the student of the history of warfare.

It was at Little Big Horn in Montana that the white men suffered their biggest defeat when, on 25 June 1876, Lieutenant-Colonel

VOLUNTEER ARMIES

Right: Officer of the 9th Cavalry in 1886.

Below: The 25th Infantry, known as 'Carpenter's Brunettes', photographed in their full dress uniform, 1880s.

Centre right: Trooper of the 2nd Cavalry in the 1888-pattern full dress.

Far right: An officer of the Honourable Artillery Company with a visiting colonel of the Ancient and Honourable Artillery Company of Boston Massachusetts, 1895.

George Custer at the head of 211 cavalrymen was surrounded and overrun by a force of Indians between 3000 and 3500 strong in the famous 'Custer's Last Stand'. Custer's defeat was largely due to his division of his forces in the face of an enemy whose numbers and fighting ability he fatally underrated. But for this fatal error, Custer might well have gone down in history as a brilliantly successful and glamorous cavalryman. At the age of twenty-three he was promoted brigadier-general with a volunteer commission and a year later he was appointed to command the 3rd Cavalry Division. During the war he had eleven horses killed under him but was only once wounded, having taken part in all the campaigns in Virginia save one.

An officer at the headquarters of the Army of the Potomac who wrote of Custer is quoted by Colonel Boatner as saying: 'He looks like a circus rider gone mad! He wears a Huzzar [sic] jacket and tight trousers of faded black velvet trimmed with tarnished gold lace . . .' He wore his hair in short, dry flaxen ringlets and, concludes his critic, 'he has a very merry blue eye and a devil-may-care style'.

His rival as 'infant prodigy' of the Northern forces was Nelson A. Miles who, having been a shop assistant before the war, commanded a division at the age of twenty-five, and remained in the regular army after peace with the rank of Colonel. After long campaigns against the Indians he found himself a Major-General and in 1895 was appointed Commander-in-Chief of the army, a position which he held during the war with Spain. He died in 1925 at the age of eighty-six.

The Spanish War has always been regarded as the arrival of the United States onto the world scene as an imperial power. Indeed, this was so, but an official United States publication described the war as having the appearance of a 'glorious national picnic'. When President McKinley called for volunteers on the outbreak of war a million men were at once forthcoming; a quarter of these were selected and their departure to the war zone was organized with no transport, no plans and no maps, and woollen uniforms for service in the tropics. Altogether it was not surprising that, while losses in action amounted to only 385 killed, deaths by disease totalled 2061.

There were two theatres of war; the Spanish possessions in the West Indies (Cuba and Puerto Rico), and the Philippine Islands. A Spanish cruiser squadron, commanded by Admiral Cervera, caused a series of panics on the east and Gulf coasts of the United States and finally based itself on Santiago in Cuba. As no movement of American troops was considered possible while the squadron was free to intervene, Santiago was blockaded by the American fleet and troops disembarked and threatened Santiago from the land. The Spanish fleet was forced out to sea where it was destroyed by the Americans in a running fight.

An armistice was arranged on 12 August and peace was signed in Paris on 10 December 1898; under its terms Cuba was placed under United States protection, though nominally an independent republic, and the Philippines became an American colonial possession.

This was immediately followed by the opening of another war, this time between the Americans and Filipino rebels, led by Emilio Aguinaldo, who had been exiled from the Islands by the Spanish authorities before the war began and had then returned with the Americans to rally the Filipinos in support of independence. Disappointed that independence was not immediately forthcoming, Aguinaldo started an uprising which lasted for six years, although he was taken prisoner half way through and retired into private life. Aguinaldo reappeared at the end of the Second World War, when he was briefly imprisoned by the government of the Philippines on suspicion of having collaborated with the Japanese. He died in 1964 at the age of ninety-four. The operations in the Philippines had furnished the United States army with its first experience of sophisticated warfare since the Civil War, and this experience was carried a stage further on the Mexican border during the years 1910 to 1916. Border raids and incidents arising out of the disturbed state of affairs within Mexico led to a concentration of American troops. In 1913, for the first time since the Civil War, a divisional headquarters was created. Hitherto troops had operated in such small units that no such grouping was necessary.

In 1916 a Mexican force crossed into United States territory at Columbus, New Mexico, killing seventeen people. As a counter measure an American force of 12,000 men under Brigadier-General John J. Pershing was despatched in pursuit of the raiders and their force was broken up after a chase of some four hundred miles.

In the same year the United States regular army doubled in strength from 128,000 to 287,000. This was the first stage in the expansion of the army to a total of over four million, which began with the declaration of war on Germany a year later, when Pershing was appointed Commander of the American Expeditionary Force in France. Like many of the senior American officers of both World Wars, Pershing had served in the Philippines. But his career was really made while he was serving as an observer with the Japanese during the Russo-Japanese War, and President Theodore Roosevelt promoted him to the rank of captain and then brigadier-general above 862 other officers.

Below: United States cavalrymen returning from the 'incident' at Wounded Knee, 1890.

147

UNITED STATES

History and traditions Until the end of the nineteenth century the American army was a small force charged with the tasks of policing its frontier and providing aid to the civil power. In war, the regular army relied upon an influx of volunteers to provide the manpower for campaigning. During the Civil War volunteers and conscription swelled the forces of both sides to a total of nearly four million, but the normal peace establishment of the army rarely exceeded 30,000 men. By the 1880s the frontier had been largely pacified and the bulk of the army was withdrawn to garrison towns and cities.

Strength The strength of the army was limited by Act of Congress and in 1899 it totalled 1775 officers and 23,364 men. The necessity to provide garrisons for Cuba, Puerto Rico and the Philippines led to a proposal to raise the peace establishment to 100,000.

Terms of service The regular army was formed of volunteers who enlisted for five years, and who were able to purchase their discharge, or be exempted from further service after three years. United States citizens were liable for service in the militia between the ages of eighteen and forty-five, and this force numbered 9300 officers and 106,251 men.

Organization The regular army was organized into twenty-five regiments of infantry each of eight companies, ten regiments of cavalry each of ten troops, five regiments of artillery each of twelve batteries, and one battalion of engineers.

In 1900, the United States army was small, scattered, and unprepared even for limited colonial warfare, but the basis for future rapid expansion was already there. Her population of seventy-six million (of which thirty-nine million were male) constituted a vast pool of manpower which Congress was not slow to tap when the need arose. Within two months of the outbreak of war with Spain in 1898, the Volunteer Army Act had provided the country with 141 regiments, twenty independent battalions, and forty-six independent companies of infantry. The experience gained in Cuba impelled the army into a programme of indoctrination which led to the adoption of many of the institutions already existing in the best European armies. The most significant of these was the formation of a professional and efficient general staff.

Above left: A typical United States infantryman during the Spanish-American War in 1898.
Above centre: A Spanish-American War trooper carrying the carbine version of the Krag rifle, 1898.
Above right: The American actor Lewis Stone with a group of comrades during the Spanish-American War, 1898.
Right: Troop L (all Indian) 1st Cavalry at sabre exercise, Fort Custer, Montana, 1892.

148

Right: An American soldier in China during the Boxer rebellion, 1900.

Opposite above left: Captain Cordell Hull, Company H, 4th Tennessee Volunteer Infantry during the Spanish-American War in 1898. He later became U.S. Secretary of State.

Opposite above right: Troopers of L Troop, 13th Cavalry, Fort Leavenworth, 1914.

Opposite below: American soldiers take it easy in their barracks, 1914.

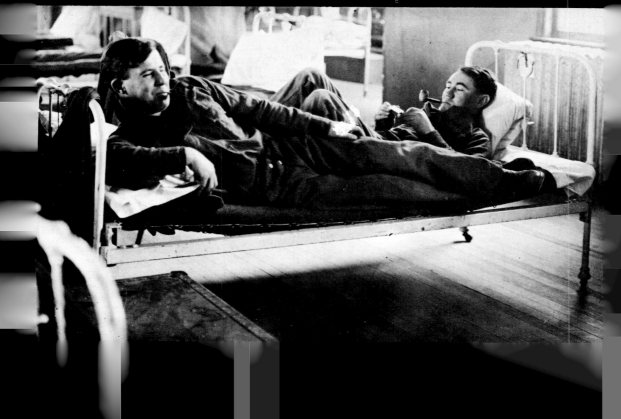

1 JAPAN

Japan started on the road to Pearl Harbor in 1811, when the army of the Shogun, the hereditary regent, received its first gun, and its first gun drill (in the Dutch language). Dutch was used because at the beginning of the seventeenth century the Japanese authorities, nervous of foreign and disloyal influences spread by priests and missionaries, had banned the landing of all foreigners in the country and had, at the same time, prevented Japanese citizens from travelling abroad. The sole exception to this rule was the permission given to the Dutch to maintain a small settlement on an island in Nagasaki harbour; an island only about 200 yards long and 80 yards wide, so small that there was no room to bury anyone on it and burials had to take place at sea. The Dutch were allowed on the mainland only once or twice a year and then had to present themselves to the Shogun with the most humiliating ritual, crawling across the throne room, called the Hall of the Hundred Mats, on their stomachs and pretending to be drunk to amuse their hosts. The Dutch, nevertheless, kept their settlement going because they found it extremely profitable to do business even under these conditions. The English had begun trading with Japan in 1613 but had abandoned their settlement ten years later.

Two hundred years after this, the tide of European expansion swelled in the China Seas and was seen by the Japanese to be threatening their country. The British took Hong Kong on the coast of China itself, while, 2000 miles away, the Russians from their settlements on the Pacific coast of Siberia began to interest themselves in the island of Sakhalin, to the north of the main Japanese archipelago. In 1853 an American squadron arrived in Japanese waters on a peaceful mission, peaceful enough but also strong enough to be able to refuse to obey when the Japanese stuck up a huge poster bearing the legend 'Depart Immediately and Dare Not Anchor' in a French translation of the original Japanese order which had been supplied by the Dutch.

These and other occurrences of the same sort rapidly brought the Japanese to the conclusion that it was necessary they should be able to resist the foreigners with their own weapons, and the Shogun issued orders that prayers should be said for the safety of the land. All that the Americans originally demanded and obtained, however, was a Japanese promise to treat well any of their shipwrecked mariners. The British, French and Dutch soon obtained the same privileges, and all gained the right to obtain supplies ashore and to anchor in the ports of Shimoda and Hakodate.

These concessions and subsequent pressure by the Western powers was enough to damage fatally the authority and prestige of the Shogun. A series of incidents ashore involving Westerners and the local Japanese authority culminated in the bombardment of Kagoshima in 1863 by a British squadron as a reprisal for the murder of a British subject. Previously the shore batteries at Shimonoseki had opened fire on American, French and Dutch ships. An allied squadron, including British ships, then bombarded the town. In this way it was made clear to the Japanese that they were

Opposite: Japanese infantry moving to the front line during the Russo-Japanese War.

virtually without any means of defence; the authority of the Shogun collapsed and the Mikado or Emperor emerged from centuries of seclusion and began once more to govern. This event is known as the Meiji Restoration.

One of the first concerns of the new Japanese authority was the provision of strong armed forces and in 1866 agreements were made with France and Britain to help develop the army and the navy. The Mikado's troops, still in their armour of iron plate and armed with bows and arrows, were sent to pacify disturbed areas where the local nobles were restless as they saw their privileges taken from them by the Emperor. The strictest orders were issued that troops were not to alarm the local population. They were not to wear blue socks, which were a sign that they were going to war, and to conciliate and to avoid provocation they were to use only the feminine forms of the language.

The Shogun and some of the local lords began individually to form the elements of an army. In some areas the local fire brigade, whose practice it was, on hearing the alarm, to march to the scene of the fire singing loudly, was the only body of men which could serve as the nucleus of the new armies.

Men were transformed into soldiers as soon as weapons and clothing could be found. The articles of clothing most needed were Western-style boots and shoes to replace the wooden sandals which were the traditional footwear. The first man to succeed in assembling a force trained on Western lines was a German sergeant named Karl Köpen, who, working for the Lord of the Kyushu clan in 1869, organized a force of 3000 trained men, with shoes, weapons, ammunition and uniforms. The language of command was German. There was tension and rivalry at this time between the German and French diplomatic missions, competing for the task of training the Japanese army, and for the influence and arms contracts that went with it.

A Franco-Japanese agreement was eventually signed on the eve of the French defeats in the war with Prussia. Despite the French loss of prestige, however, their mission to Japan lasted for some time. The only traces of it now are in the pictures of the uniforms worn in the first war with China (1894-5) and the full dress uniform worn by the Emperor today.

Compulsory military service was introduced in 1872, a revolution as great as any brought about by the opening of Japan to Western ideas. Hitherto fighting had been the privilege of the Samurai, professional hereditary soldiers, and the ordinary man in the street or the field was considered too lowly to enjoy that privilege. Apart from concern at this great break with tradition there were other doubts, for it was feared that, in the event of civil unrest, the conscripts would take the side of the workers and peasants.

In 1874 the first Japanese expeditionary force of modern days sailed to Formosa to obtain reparation for the ill-treatment of shipwrecked Japanese mariners at the hands of the Chinese authorities then ruling the island. The expedition was, however, badly managed. Chinese resistance was stronger than anticipated and British diplomatic intervention was necessary to extricate the Japanese from the embarrassment in which they had involved themselves.

Two years later came the last of the Japanese civil wars with the revolt of the powerful Satsuma clan in protest against the loss of their inherited privileges under the new Meiji regime. In this struggle the government forces amounted to about 66,000 and those of the Satsuma 40,000. The losses of the two sides totalled 35,000 or one-third of all those engaged. The most important factor in the fighting was that the Samurai were life-long professional soldiers and the government forces were the new conscripts, drawn from all classes of the people. The government victory showed clearly that their army was being developed in the right direction. It showed too that a fighting spirit was not an exclusive possession of the Samurai, for it was clear that, if well led, all Japanese could fight with the same fervour. Nevertheless there was a long way to go before the Japanese army reached a reasonable standard of efficiency, as was shown in 1880. At the beginning of the 1880s the army's peace-time strength was 35,000, with 53,000 reserves, and it was decided to experiment with the holding of manoeuvres on a large scale. The first results, according to foreign observers, were shocking, and those of the second series of manoeuvres held in the following year were declared to be even worse. There appeared to be no understanding of command above battalion level.

Great changes were introduced; the French mission was brought to an end and replaced by a German one, headed by one of the greatest military teachers of the nineteenth century, a German colonel named Meckel. Meckel not only trained the Japanese army but, at the German staff college, taught Ludendorff, Seeckt and Groener, three of the most famous of the German generals of the First World War.

At this time a great wave of economy ran through the Japanese Ministry of War. Civil servants were in future to be given only hot water instead of tea and, during the fiercely cold Japanese winter, they were no longer issued with hot coals for their Hibatchi braziers, their only means of keeping warm. (It is unlikely that Meckel was responsible for these measures of austerity for he was, it would seem, a cheerful man whose favourite relaxation was drinking Moselle wine.) Under the German's care the army grew; in 1884 brigades were introduced and exercised for the first time, and two years later divisions were formed.

Meckel understood the great importance of the use of the newly introduced railways and of keeping roads in good condition. At that time the Japanese navy was still very small and he realized that the army would have to await attack and then move with the greatest speed to meet an enemy landing. However, in the spring of 1890, he also began practising combined operations.

The German mission came to an end in 1894, just as Japan was preparing for its first foreign war in modern times, against China.

This was the first of three wars to be fought within the next sixty years for command of Korea. To secure rights which they believed to be theirs, both China and Japan sent troops to that country, the Japanese to the south around Seoul and the Chinese to the north. In a series of notes, charges, and counter-charges China claimed that Korea stood in a special relationship to her and that it was therefore China's business to effect the reforms for which Japan was pressing. This was denied by Japan, who announced that she was going to carry out the reforms that she held necessary. War was declared on 1 August 1894, but fighting had already broken out on 25 July when the Japanese army opened an attack. Both China and Japan depended upon seaborne communications for the supply of their armies. The Japanese thus secured an important success when a British-owned steamer, the *Kowshing,* chartered by the Chinese government to carry troops to Korea, was sunk, also on 25 July, by a Japanese cruiser commanded by the future Admiral Togo, victor of Tsushima. More than one thousand Chinese soldiers lost their lives.

On 17 September the Japanese and Chinese fleets met off the mouth of the Yalu and, although the Japanese were unable to secure a decisive victory, the Chinese fleet took no further part in the war. The Japanese were able to exploit their success. They crossed the Yalu River, penetrated into Manchuria and, by amphibious operations, took the strategically vital bases of Port Arthur (on 21 November) and Wei-hai-wei. Following the surrender of Wei-hai-wei on 12 February, when the Chinese commander Admiral Ting and a number of his officers took poison, the Japanese prepared to advance on Peking. Seven divisions were concentrated at Port Arthur, intending to land at Shan-hai-kwan, 170 miles from the Chinese capital.

Japanese forces occupied the Pescadores and Formosa, but before the landings could take place at Shan-hai-kwan the Chinese surrendered and a peace treaty was signed at Shimonoseki on 17 April 1895.

The reaction of the European great powers to the Japanese success was immediate. Russia, Germany and France 'recommended' that Port Arthur should be returned to China in the interests of peace. Japan was exhausted financially; her ships had been continuously at sea for the past eight months and her reserves of raw materials were at an end. There was nothing for it but to carry out the 'recommendation' of the three powers and return Port Arthur to China. Within twenty years, when the Japanese demanded the surrender of the German base at Tsingtao in August 1914, they copied exactly the wording of the 'recommendation' which the Germans, and their allies, the French and the Russians, had tendered them in 1895. Three years later, in 1898, the Russians, who had pledged themselves not to seize Port Arthur, did so.

In 1900, on the outbreak of the Boxer Rising, Japan, being the nearest to the scene of trouble, was able to send two infantry divisions to the relief of the foreign legations besieged in Peking.

Having obtained what they hoped to be a free hand in Korea, the

Japanese were, reasonably enough, disappointed when they saw the Russians moving into the area from which they had just ejected the Chinese. Their economy had by no means recovered from the strains put upon it by the war with China and they were anxious to avoid a fresh conflict. To achieve this, Russo-Japanese negotiations were carried on over a period of months, based on a Japanese proposal that Korea should be divided into two spheres of interest, Russian and Japanese, separated by the 39th parallel, with the Russians taking the northern half of the country and the Japanese the southern. (The 39th parallel, it will be remembered, was also the dividing line agreed between the Russian and American zones of occupation and re-established in 1953 as the boundary between North and South Korea.)

In 1904, negotiations between Russia and Japan had been in progress for some seven months, when the Japanese navy carried out a surprise attack on the Russian Pacific fleet at Port Arthur on 8 February. This attack did sufficient damage to put the Russians temporarily out of action, assuring the Japanese of command of the sea, a command of which they took instant advantage, landing troops on the Asian mainland, at Chemulpo. Historians emphasize the great care with which the Japanese made their preparations. This was their army's first war against a European enemy, and it was essential that everything should go well.

Accordingly it was not until 1 May that the Japanese were ready to cross the Yalu. Once across, the army divided into two parts; the

Japanese soldiers with weapons captured from the Chinese Boxers during the uprising in 1900.

Above: Japanese Major Yamaoka in his quarters at the end of the siege of Port Arthur.

Right: General Nogi and his staff take lunch before Port Arthur.

Opposite: Field-Marshal Oyama, Commander-in-Chief of the Japanese forces in Manchuria, c. 1905. French influence is apparent in the rank distinction braids on the cuffs of his frock coat.

main body under Marshal Oyama followed the Russian main body under General Kuropatkin as it fell back northward towards Mukden in Southern Manchuria, while the Japanese Third Army, under General Nogi, crossed the Liao-Tung peninsula, thus cutting off Port Arthur and beginning a siege on 5 May. There now followed a period of inactivity while the Japanese waited for the siege to take effect and the Russians in Manchuria waited for reinforcements by land and by sea. With extraordinary dilatoriness and inefficiency, a Second Pacific Squadron was being assembled in the Baltic, which was to sail half way round the world to join the First Pacific Squadron at Port Arthur. Each of these Russian fleets was, in theory, just a little weaker than the combined Japanese fleet; together they were much more powerful. It therefore became essential for the Japanese to capture Port Arthur and, if possible, destroy the First Pacific Squadron before the Second could reach the Far East.

On 10 August the First Squadron, commanded by Admiral Witgeft, left Port Arthur for Vladivostock, fearing that if it remained any longer at Port Arthur it could be put out of action by the shore-based Japanese heavy artillery (eleven-inch howitzers). Once outside its base, however, it was attacked by Togo's fleet, which had maintained a blockade since the beginning of the war, and was driven back into port again. By mid-August it was clear that the siege of Port Arthur was not progressing fast enough and that the Russian Second Squadron might win the race. The Japanese, therefore, decided that Port Arthur would have to be subjected to an all-out assault and this was begun by Nogi on 19 August.

While the Japanese Third Army was fighting hard at Port Arthur, 175 miles to the north-east Kuropatkin was concentrating an army, 100,000 strong, at Liao Yang. He was waiting for reinforcements from Europe and withstanding a Japanese attack

designed eventually to take Mukden some thirty-five miles further up the railway. Although inferior in strength, the Japanese drove the Russians slowly northwards. But Kuropatkin was an able general when on the defensive and was able to disengage his army and began to plan an offensive battle of his own on the Sha Ho River. The battle lasted fourteen days and developed on a thirty-seven-mile front. The outcome was a Russian failure and Kuropatkin's consequent withdrawal from the battle was a discouragement to the Russians in the field and to the civil population and government at home. Bad weather brought the fighting to an end on a line fifteen miles south of Mukden, and both sides dug in for the winter with a lavish use of barbed wire (a forecast of developments on the Western Front ten years later).

The fighting outside Port Arthur was now coming to a climax; on 5 December the Japanese stormed 203 Metre Hill, the key to the whole Russian position, to the town and to the harbour. From this hill the Japanese artillery was able to open direct fire on the Russian warships and pick them off one by one. After some of the fiercest fighting in history, in which Nogi lost 58,000 killed and wounded, and 34,000 sick, the fortress surrendered on 2 January 1905.

There remained two more acts of this drama of the Russo-Japanese War. First came the Japanese advance on Mukden and the final land-battle of the war fought there between 21 February and 10 March. Oyama, reinforced by Nogi's army, which had been freed by the surrender of Port Arthur, and by a new army (the Fifth) from Japan made up of reservists and recruits, was now commanding 300,000 men, and he began an attack on a front of nearly fifty miles. The Russian army was about the same strength. This total involvement of 600,000 men gave Mukden the honour of being the biggest battle in history — a title which it was to lose within ten years.

Both the Russians and the Japanese were planning to attack, but the Japanese struck first and, although they were equal in strength to the Russians, they were able to stretch their line and so hold the Russians in the middle, while outflanking them at both extremities of their position. On the western flank, Nogi's Third Army worked round behind Mukden, threatening the railway which was the Russians' line of retreat. The Russians succeeded in holding it open long enough for what was left of their army to fall back towards Harbin, but Mukden was lost and with it about half the Russian army, killed, wounded or taken prisoner. Japanese losses were over 40,000. After the fall of Port Arthur disjointed attempts at peace were made internationally to bring about an end to the war.

However, as long as their fleet from the Baltic was making its way, very slowly, around the world, the Russians believed that they still had a chance of victory. It was not until that fleet had been wiped out in the Straits of Tsushima by the Japanese fleet under Togo that they agreed to treat. The peace conference, organized by President Theodore Roosevelt, met at Portsmouth, New Hampshire and the treaty was signed on 5 September 1905.

JAPAN

History and traditions After two and a half
centuries of feudal isolation, during which all
military institutions had been the sole preserve of
the aristocracy and the Samurai, Japan was faced in
the 1860s with the need to develop a modern mass
army to resist the aggressive commercialism of the
West. The collapse of the Shogunate and the
restoration of the Emperor allowed General
Yamagata Aritomo to reorganize the army. He was
faced by considerable opposition, particularly from
the two million members of the Samurai class whose
claim to form the new army was rejected in favour of
universal conscription. Yamagata had studied the
French and Prussian armies and he quickly
established a military academy, several military
schools, and a general staff based on the Prussian
model. In 1883 the army was organized as six
national divisions, and one guards division which
provided an Imperial bodyguard. The work begun by
Yamagata was continued by Oyama Iwao, the
leading member of the Satsuma clan, who had been
an observer during the Franco-Prussian War and
who rose to the rank of field-marshal.

Strength Even when fully mobilized, the Japanese
army was small by European standards. At the end
of the Sino-Japanese War in 1895 the army
numbered 70,000 active troops with a reserve of
200,000. By the outbreak of the Russo-Japanese War
in 1904 the Japanese had a front line strength of
180,000 men, and a further 400,000 divided equally
between the first and second reserves.

Terms of service The liability for service extended
to all males between the ages of seventeen and forty.
After three years service with the active army, the
soldier passed into the first reserve for four years four
months, and then into the second reserve for a
further five years.

Officers Officers received a thoroughly professional
training in the military colleges and the academy,
and many were given the opportunity of studying in
France, Germany and Great Britain. The officer
corps played an active and often disruptive role in the
formulation of national policy, and the army rebelled
against government decisions in 1874, 1876 and
1877.

Organization The highest tactical formation in the
army was the division, consisting of two brigades
each of two infantry regiments and one regiment or
battalion of cavalry with supporting troops. Field
armies were usually formed of three divisions giving
a total strength of approximately 40,000 men. In
1900 there were twenty-eight regiments of infantry,
seven regiments of cavalry, six regiments of field
artillery, four regiments of coast artillery, and six
battalions of pioneers.

The Japanese army's meteoric rise to world
importance was achieved largely on the basis of a
strong national will guided by a number of soldiers of
outstanding professional commitment. The financial
base of the army was insecure and only a fraction of
the men liable to service could be enrolled and
trained. After six months of fighting in 1904, the
army was engaged in a desperate attempt to raise
and train its men, and although 1,100,000 men
served with the colours only 400,000 were fit for
combat duty.

*Field-Marshal Oku. As commanding general of the
2nd Army, Oku landed his army at Quantung, and
then proceeded to participate with distinction in most
of the engagements of the Russo-Japanese War.*

2 CHINA

The most costly war in terms of human life, in all history, was called by those who fought in it 'the Great Peace'. This term is reminiscent of some of the expressions used by Big Brother in Orwell's *1984* and one which, in its Chinese form *Tai Ping,* is still used.

Twenty million people were killed in this war between 1850 and 1864 and, while the Chinese fought amongst themselves, European powers, notably Britain, France and Russia, took full advantage to extract by force or threats of force commercial and territorial concessions. It was this use of force, costing a few thousand Chinese and European lives, which is remembered now by both sides rather than the events which began the war. In 1850 Hung Hsiu Chuan announced that he was the younger brother of Jesus Christ and was going to reform the land and right the many wrongs in China. Hung and his three brothers, known collectively as 'the Four Hung Princes', destroyed their private property, gave all their goods to be shared and attracted a great following. Hung's first army was described by its enemies as 'Ten Thousand Long-Haired Bandits', because they were forbidden to cut their hair. They proclaimed the abolition of prostitution, the sale of slaves, the binding of women's feet, opium smoking, adultery, witchcraft, gambling and the use of tobacco and wine.

China's transition from military feudalism to modern military science is illustrated in this picture of a Chinese war-lord inspecting a Gatling gun.

In the cause of these reforms thousands upon thousands were mercilessly slaughtered, but Hung's puritanical zeal was soon dissipated. In 1853 he proclaimed himself Emperor Tien Wang and is said to have led a carefree existence in the seclusion of his palace attended by numerous concubines.

Nevertheless Hung's armies carried his dominions far and wide. In the north they reached Tientsin, and in the east they took Nanking, the second city of China, which they held for twelve years and which became their capital.

In 1859 came what has been called the Second Opium War. The great value of the Chinese markets to the Western powers made Europeans extremely anxious to force their wares upon the Chinese. The British and French, acting together, occupied Canton in 1857 and then attacked the Taku fortifications at the mouth of the Peiho on the road to Peking, the Chinese capital. However, a British landing at Taku was defeated on 25 June 1859. The most famous incident of this battle was the conduct of the American Commodore Josiah Tatnall who, although officially neutral, sent his boats into the Chinese fire to pick up the crews of sunken British boats, remarking that blood was thicker than water.

The next year the British and French renewed the attack, the British establishing a base at an uninhabited spot on the Liao-Tung peninsula which they named Port Arthur after Lieutenant Arthur of H.M.S. *Algerine,* who first hoisted the Union Jack there in 1860.

After the capture of Taku, 10,500 British and 6300 French troops advanced on Peking, where the Imperial Palace was sacked by the

French as a reprisal for the murder of a missionary; peace terms were then settled.

Reflecting on the qualities of the enemy's troops which had been shown during this war, the British sharply distinguished between two classes; the Chinese and the Manchus. All regular or semi-regular troops of the Emperor were organized as 'bannermen', according to the colour of the banners under which they were grouped. Chinese bannermen seemed little interested in the war and were unwilling to face attack. But the Manchu bannermen fought bravely, apparently believing they were fighting for their lives and for the Manchu dynasty, which was unpopular with its Chinese subjects. The unpopularity of the Manchu dynasty was one of the reasons why the Chinese failed to check the advance of the Taiping Rebellion whose forces, at their greatest strength, numbered a million disciplined and fanatical soldiers, divided into men's and women's divisions.

The rebellion was spreading across central China during the 1850s, and by the end of the decade it was threatening Shanghai, the principal centre of Western trade. The merchants there were alarmed and formed a kind of unofficial foreign legion, called the 'Ever Victorious Army', commanded by a twenty-eight-year-old American, Frederick Townsend Ward, from Salem, Massachusetts. The 'Army' consisted of about one hundred foreigners, mostly discharged seamen or deserters from the British and French forces which were gathering for the expedition against Peking. Its first operation, against the town of Sung Kiang, the Taiping's nearest point to Shanghai, failed completely and Ward disbanded what was left of his force. He formed another troop of Filipinos from Manila, which was successful at Sung Kiang, and then had two failures against the town of Ching Pu. Ward was severely wounded, arrested by the foreign authorities in Shanghai and imprisoned for encouraging desertion. On his release he made a third attempt to form an army, this time with ten foreign officers and between 4000 and 8000 trained and disciplined Chinese. When the Taiping rebels threatened Shanghai, Ward's force, together with foreign troops and those of the Chinese government, successfully defended the town, but Ward was mortally wounded during the fighting.

Charles Gordon, a captain in the Royal Engineers, was seconded by the British government to take his place and, in all, the Ever Victorious Army won more than a hundred engagements on the Yangtse thanks in part to skilful use of amphibious tactics. 'Chinese' Gordon was killed twenty years later at Khartoum.

The Taiping Rebellion was ended in 1864 and Tien Wang committed suicide. The Manchus continued in power despite several rebellions, amounting in some cases almost to civil wars, and in addition fought a kind of quasi-war with France. This originated in operations by the French in Indo-China, one of a number of territories which were semi-possessions of China. At this time the maximum strength of the Chinese army was eight Manchu banners, described as 'the largest and most useless of formations', plus sixteen more banners made up of Mongols and Chinese allies, while the Army of the Green Standard served as a decentralized constabulary and was less mobile. There were, however, the beginnings of a more sophisticated force, including a few thousand bannermen forming the Peking Field Force and other selected constabulary units.

A German mission had trained and now led the 3000 men of 'the Self-Strengthening Army' at Nanking, but eventually Japanese instructors replaced the Germans on grounds of economy. One of the odd by-products of this was that Chiang Kai Shek, after a year at the Chinese military academy, passed into the equivalent Japanese establishment.

Apart from Chiang Kai Shek there emerged at this time two other men who were to have a decisive influence on the future of China: Yuan Shih Kai, the commander at Tientsin of the 7000 men of the Peiyang Army, tried to make himself Emperor of China in 1916 but was powerfully dissuaded by the Japanese with British and French support; and Sun Yat Sen, who became leader of the Chinese Revolution. He had been taught medicine and cricket by Sir James Cantlie who also prevented him from being literally Shanghaied by the Chinese Legation in London.

Although the prevailing picture of China for the newspaper reader of the time was one of war lords, civil wars and bandits, a certain amount was accomplished by what central government there was. In the extreme west, towards Turkestan, the boundaries of the Empire were pushed further afield until they met those of Russia in Turkestan. At the other end of the Empire, in the area now known as Vietnam, there was a dispute over another of China's tributary states, Tonking. The French wished to secure the use of the ports of Hanoi and Haiphong as bases for economic penetration into the Chinese province of Yunnan. Fighting started at Langson on 21 June 1884, when a French attack was repulsed. In support of the army, the French fleet, under Admiral Courbet, raided the Chinese naval base at Foochow and landed on Formosa intending to destroy the coal mines. They were driven off but did succeed in stopping the rice trade between Formosa and the mainland. The importance of this trade was such that its cessation forced the Chinese government to make peace on condition that the French withdrew from Formosa and the Pescadores.

All in all, the Chinese came out of these encounters with some credit, and their success gave them and the European powers an exaggerated idea of what, under other circumstances, they were able to achieve. This was proved all too plainly by the results of the Sino-Japanese War of 1894-5.

On their way to fight this war the Chinese troops were not an impressive sight. A Scotswoman, Isabella Bird, saw them passing through the old Tartar city of Mukden on their way to Korea on 1 August 1894, and her biographer wrote:

They looked the losers they would be, she thought. Their clothes were stagey and unserviceable — loose-sleeved red jackets, blue or apricot trousers, boots of thick black cotton cloth, their weapons were of mainly historical value — muzzle loading muskets, spears and bayonets, and their general impedimenta were medieval — paper fans and umbrellas, banners and singing birds tethered to sticks. It was a sad colourful pageant shambling loosely through the muddy streets.

Mrs Bird commented: 'It was nothing but murder to send thousands of men so armed *to meet the Japanese.*'

In addition, the supply services of the Chinese army were monuments of corruption and inefficiency. Commanders stole their men's pay, sold their rations when any were available, and accepted for their financial gain inferior or useless ammunition.

For the Japanese, on the other hand, what was happening was a well-organized, and well-carried out, rehearsal for the war with Russia which began ten years later. Tactics included landings in Korea, an advance to the Yalu, then, the river once crossed, one part of the army cutting off Port Arthur while the other sought a more distant goal, Peking in 1895, Mukden in 1905.

Just as it was necessary for the Japanese to gain command of the sea in 1904 before they could start large-scale military operations, so it was necessary in 1894 for them to defeat the Chinese fleet. They did this off the mouth of the Yalu on 14 September and followed up their success with landings near Port Arthur on 24 October. The Chinese offered little resistance and the Japanese then mounted a successful combined operation against Wei-hai-wei, the principal Chinese naval base, on the opposite side of the Gulf of Chih Li on 19 January 1895. As the attack on Peking was being prepared, Li Hung Chang appeared with Chinese peace proposals, and a treaty was signed at Shimonoseki on 17 April 1895. As we have seen, Port Arthur had to be returned to China, but Japanese troops occupied Formosa and the Pescadores Islands, between Formosa and the mainland, and this occupation was followed by annexation which lasted until 1945.

Now two tides of discontent were rising in China; the country's rulers were bitterly criticized for permitting foreigners to seize Chinese territory and for outraging Chinese customs which dated from times long before the keeping of records. The famous Dowager Empress and her ministers took advantage of this situation by first claiming, clandestinely, that the foreigners were responsible for everything that was going wrong. They then turned to the foreigners, and deplored the excesses of the discontented Chinese, which they were unwilling to do anything to check. The most extreme manifestations of discontent were produced by a society organized, in theory, to promote physical culture, the Society of Patriotic Harmonious Fists, nicknamed the Boxers.

The centre of the Boxer movement was the capital Peking, and the behaviour of the Boxers led Sir Claude MacDonald, the British Minister, doyen of the Diplomatic Corps, to ask the governments with forces in Far Eastern waters to provide protection. The forces immediately available consisted of landing parties from the ships

Types of Chinese soldiers in Peking, 1900.

which had gathered off the Taku forts and the advance on Peking had to be made by rail. A party of some four hundred seamen and marines of seven nationalities (British, French, German, Austrian, American, Italian and Japanese) was assembled and set off for the Chinese capital, which it reached just in time to prevent the foreign legations being overrun. However, it was soon clear that the original four hundred would not be enough to enable the legations to hold out and that the despatch of a relief column would be necessary. Under the command of the British admiral, Sir Edward Seymour, this second force of two thousand men, drawn from the original seven nationalities together with a Russian detachment, began to advance up the railway by way of Tientsin on 9 June 1900. However, by 14 June it was stopped by larger Boxer forces and eventually had to fall back on Tientsin where it was cut off, unable to advance or to retire.

The successful resistance of the Chinese came as a surprise to their enemies. But the Boxers had been indoctrinated with the belief that they were either invulnerable or that, if they were killed, they would be able to resurrect themselves at nightfall. Allied rifle and machine gun fire cut lanes through the advancing crowd, armed for the most part only with swords and pikes. Their leaders danced and sang before them to encourage them, as they prepared to go through the ritual designed to make them safe from the bullets which were killing them.

The troops of the regular Imperial Chinese army at first remained neutral. The Boxers on occasion removed the bullets from this army's cartridges so that, if they did attack, they would be firing blanks, which would do nothing but enhance the reputation for invulnerability of the Boxers. Eventually, some of the regular units in the area joined the Boxers, but they never fought with the same total disregard for death.

It became clear to Western powers that a much bigger force would be needed to reach Peking. This was raised from all over the Far East, from places as far apart as India and Siberia, assembling an international force of 20,000 men. Back in Germany, the Kaiser

ARMIES OF THE FAR EAST

Right: A Boxer standard-bearer, Peking 1900.

Below: Chinese loyalist artillery during the Boxer Rebellion, 1900.

Opposite above: Chinese infantryman, Peking 1900.

Opposite below: Loyal Chinese troops guard an allied troop train in China during the Boxer Rebellion, 1900.

Opposite: Soldiers of the new Chinese Republican army in 1912. Note the pigtails worn in the regulation manner in the pocket.

decided to mount an impressive propaganda spectacle by sending large forces to China with a blood-curdling exhortation to remember the deeds of their ancestor Attila. This speech was the origin of the term 'Huns' given to the Germans in the First World War by their enemies. In fact, the German contingent did not reach China until the end of September and the relief of the legations had been carried out by the original 20,000 men on 14 August 1900.

The policy of the Chinese government during the siege of the legations is a puzzle which has remained unsolved to this day. The Dowager Empress had agreed, on the urging of some of her most conservative nobles, to order the attack on the legations. However, she and her advisers seem almost to have been afraid lest it succeed — perhaps because success might have so increased the extreme conservative influence as to rob the Dowager Empress of her authority.

The difference between the Chinese and Japanese reactions to the Western challenge in the latter half of the nineteenth century is striking. In China there was silent acquiescence to the deeds of the foreign invader, interrupted occasionally by fanatical resistance backed with obsolete weapons. In Japan, once the first resistance had been overcome, there followed an equally fanatical determination to learn from the technology and skills of the newcomers.

The basic difference between the two approaches seems to have been that, from time immemorial, soldiering in Japan had been a highly esteemed and much admired profession. It will be recalled that in the centuries when the Shoguns ruled, only the envied, favoured and hereditary few, the Samurai, were allowed to bear arms.

In China, on the other hand, soldiering was poorly regarded. Soldiers were the lowest and most miserable of men and joined the ranks of the armies of the various local war lords because they were forced to, or because it was the only alternative to a life of unsuccessful beggary and theft. The armies of the war lords were completely corrupt, the rewards growing greater with each rung of the ladder of promotion. There was generally no appeal to patriotism or to religious feeling, although, as has been seen both in the Taiping Rebellion and the Boxer Rising, appeals were made and were answered with a breathtaking readiness for self-immolation.

As late as 1941, before the war between China and Japan had been expanded by the attack on Pearl Harbor, an American correspondent visiting the front reported that she had met a soldier to whom she had put the question; 'Whose soldier are you?', expecting to get in reply the name of the local commander. She was surprised and pleased by the answer; 'I am China's soldier.' But that sentiment came too late and was felt by too few. The corruption of the last years of Chiang Kai Shek stifled most of the sparks which had been kindled. During the Korean War ten years later, it was clear that the coming of Communism created a disciplined fanaticism which neither the old Empire nor the Republic of the war lords and of Chiang Kai Shek had been able to achieve.

CHINA

History and traditions In the nineteenth century China did not possess a national regular army in the European sense of the term. The Manchu troops of the Eight Banners had provided garrisons for Peking and chief provincial centres since the early seventeenth century, but only the 20,000 men of the Peking Field Force would be able to make a sustained contribution in any military operation. The campaign against the Taiping rebels in 1860-4 led to the creation of an Imperial army financed by the merchants of Shanghai. In recognition of the successful leadership of its first commander, an American named Frederick Ward, the force was given the title of the 'Ever Victorious Army'. Ward's death in the assault on the city of Tzeki led to the appointment of Captain Charles G. Gordon of the Royal Engineers as the army's commanding officer. Gordon's superiors hoped that once the Taipings had been destroyed the Ever Victorious Army would become the nucleus of a regular Chinese army. Unfortunately Gordon, who twice had to deal with mutinies amongst the army's officers, disbanded the force on his own initiative once the Taipings had been crushed. He then attached himself as an instructor to the Imperialist forces and trained the Manchu armies for five months.

Organization Until the reorganization of the Chinese army after the Boxer Rebellion, the principal troops of the Empire were formed as two distinct corps; that of the Eight Banners and that of the Green Standard. The Manchu troops of the Eight Banners were in a sense a federal force which was outside the control of provincial military officials. In contrast, the men of the Green Standard were a militia force provided from contingents levied from each province. There was no structure for the overall command of the provincial forces in war, and their use outside their own areas does not seem to have been contemplated. Every province was responsible for recruiting a contingent of 35,000 men, of whom the majority was untrained and equipped with obsolete weapons. The nominal strength of the provincial forces was approximately 500,000 men, but the actual strength was little more than 150,000, and their duties were more those of a police force than of a military unit.

It was not until after the Russo-Japanese War that China was able to make any progress towards the organization of a modern national army. A decree of 1905 provided, in theory, for the establishment of an officer training college, and a number of cadet schools, and a genuine, though only partially successful, attempt was made to form an army responsible solely to the central government. The Army of the Green Standard was placed under the control of the Minister of War in 1907, and by 1909 a northern army of six divisions and one brigade had been organized, with a further three divisions and six brigades serving in the rest of the Empire.

IV·THE DETERRENT THAT WORKS

SWITZERLAND

In a short survey of the principal armies of the world and their development between 1854 and 1914 the Swiss army may seem out of place. Its strength, completely mobilized in 1914, was just over half a million, compared with the great European armies which numbered over four million each on mobilization and all of which increased their strength by millions more as the war went on. Moreover, the Swiss army was not a standing army but a militia force, of which a proportion was called up for a few weeks training each year. Apart from those few weeks there were no troops ready for action. Nevertheless, the Swiss army has played a vital part, not only in the defence of its country but also in the history of Europe during the past 150 years.

In the 1840s, however, things were very different. The Swiss Confederation had only comparatively recently been reassembled by the Congress of Vienna after occupation and annexation by Napoleon and neighbouring countries had seen this rebirth with little enthusiasm. France, Austria, Piedmont and Prussia would all have welcomed the collapse of the Confederation so that they could profit from its partition.

The Confederation, as re-established at Vienna, was a much less tightly knit affair than it is today, and in the 1840s a strong movement grew up, notably in the Protestant, and more liberal, cantons to strengthen the authority of the central government, which was opposed by the Catholic and more conservative cantons. After much debate, some rioting, notably in Geneva, and local elections, the twenty-two cantons of the Confederation divided in 1847: thirteen Protestant to seven Catholic with two neutral. The Catholic group, which called itself the Sonderbund, claimed that the dissolution of the monasteries by the canton of Aargau was a violation of the guaranty of religious liberty promised by the Treaty of Vienna. Aargau retorted that the religious orders had been undermining the civilian administration.

France, Prussia, Piedmont and Austria intervened in defence of the Treaty of Vienna and asked for British support. Palmerston, then Foreign Secretary, carefully delayed a reply to the notes of the powers, a favourite tactic of his when he was anxious to avoid doing anything. Faced by the British delay, the Continental powers postponed taking action and the Swiss Federal government acted to put down the Sonderbund before there could be any interventions from outside.

An army 100,000 strong, commanded by a Genevese officer, General W. H. Dufour, was assembled by the Federal government; the Sonderbund mobilized 70,000 men under Colonel J. U. von Salis-Soglio. Both commanders were veterans of the armies of Napoleon.

Dufour struck first; of the seven cantons of the Sonderbund six lay together in a single bloc, while the seventh, Fribourg, lay apart. Within a few days Dufour's troops had surrounded the separate canton and compelled it to surrender on 14 November. They then moved against the main force of the Sonderbund. The two armies

Opposite above: Swiss artillery at gunnery practice, c. 1910.

Below: A machine gun ready to fire during Swiss army manoeuvres. The white band on the shako denoted the enemy, c. 1910.

met at the little town of Gislikon near Lucerne, and in a brief action the Federal forces stormed the enemy position. Casualties on both sides were small; the Federal troops lost 78 killed and 280 wounded and the Sonderbund 50 killed and 175 wounded. The resistance of the Sonderbund collapsed and the war ended after nineteen days.

Since then the Swiss army has never fought, but it has been mobilized four times, in 1856-57, 1870, 1914 and 1939, to protect the country's neutrality. The army's success in doing this is, of course, the justification for its existence. At first sight the claim that the Germans in two world wars were deterred from invading Switzerland by the Swiss army seems very much exaggerated. The basis for the claim, however, does not rest upon a comparison of the strengths of the German and Swiss armies, which in both wars was about ten million against half a million, but on the difficulties of the terrain which confronts an invader of Switzerland and the high standard of training reached by the Swiss. This made it clear that it was a great deal easier to attack France through the Low Countries than through Switzerland. That resistance would be serious was a fact of which the Germans were convinced without it ever having been put

to the test. In a sense it was a propaganda triumph for the Swiss, its basis being the belief in their determination to resist and the reputation they had as riflemen. Every male Swiss had to belong to a rifle club, of which there were nearly 4000 in the country, and to reach a certain standard of marksmanship every year, paying a tax if he were not successful. This was even more important then than now because the development of weaponry up to 1914 and later was such that the principal weapon in Alpine warfare was the rifle.

Ancient chestnuts are sometimes worth resurrecting as they may illustrate public belief at the time they were in circulation. For years before 1914 the story was current of an inspection by the Kaiser of a great parade by the Swiss army, with 10,000 men present. A Swiss soldier was presented to the Imperial guest who said the usual polite things and then asked: 'You have 10,000 men here. What would you do if I came against you with 10,000 men?'

'Your Imperial Majesty, every one of us would fire once.'

'And if I came against you with 20,000 men?'

'We would fire twice.'

SWITZERLAND

History and traditions Switzerland's strategic position as a potential invasion route between France, Italy, Austria or Germany has been the dominant reason both for her traditional neutrality and for the maintenance of her unique national army. The first Confederation of Swiss States in 1291 was essentially a military pact of mutual support and its members pursued their struggle for national freedom with a ruthless disregard of military convention. In battles such as Näfels (1388), St Jacob (1444) and Morat (1476) their infantry earned a reputation as the finest soldiers in Europe. The tradition of fierce military professionalism was carried into the nineteenth century by the Swiss troops in the service of Napoleon I and their battle fought on the Beresina (1812) passed into national legend.

With the establishment of her neutrality by the Second Paris Peace Treaty (1815) Switzerland became determined to defend her territorial integrity against any aggressor, and her troops were mobilized during the winter of 1856-7 when Prussia threatened war and during the Franco-German War of 1870-1.

Strength In 1900, from a population of just over 3,300,000 the Swiss cantons could call upon an army of 238,244 fully trained men all under the age of forty-five. Their total military budget for the year was £1,124,836.

System of recruiting The Swiss army was a militia force recruited by obligatory service and organized on the German system. The only personnel permanently on service were 240 officers employed as instructors, and approximately 100 garrison guards who were all tradesmen charged with the repair of fortifications. The recruits' initial training lasted from forty-seven days in the infantry to eighty-two days in the cavalry and refresher courses, which were held annually for cavalry and in alternate years for other arms, varied from twelve to eighteen days. Upon joining the army, the majority of recruits were already skilled at arms and drill through membership of one of the country's numerous rifle clubs and cadet corps. The cantons were responsible for the recruitment of the infantry and the majority of the cavalry and artillery, while the Confederation recruited for the engineers and medical services.

Terms of service Every citizen was liable to military service for a period of twenty-five years, normally starting at the age of twenty. This service was divided into first year recruits' training, twelve years in the Élite or active army, and twelve years in the Landwehr. In addition, all able-bodied men between the ages of seventeen and fifty were liable for service in the Landsturm. Those citizens who were exempted from duty with the Élite and Landwehr were required to pay an annual tax, consisting of a personal levy of six francs and a supplementary tax in proportion to property or income.

Officers All officers had to pass through the ranks and only after the completion of NCO courses were suitable candidates sent for officer training, their actual commission being dependent upon success in a competitive examination.

Organization For the purposes of command, manoeuvres, and war the army was organized as a field force of four army corps, each of two divisions plus supporting troops; the garrisons of the St Gothard and St Maurice defences; and a reserve of 3000 Élite, 35,000 Landwehr, and 277,000 Landsturm.

Infantry An infantry battalion consisted of four companies of 176 men and five officers and there were twelve battalions to each army division.

Cavalry Cavalry regiments comprised three squadrons of 119 men and four officers and there were two regiments serving with each division.

Artillery The artillery was divided into field batteries, mountain batteries, position artillery companies, fortress artillery companies, and machine gun companies. There was no horse artillery and its place was taken by sections of cavalry machine guns.

Engineers The engineers were organized in the following sections; sappers, pontoniers, fortress sappers, and pioneers. The sappers comprised sixteen Élite companies, the pontoniers two Élite companies and four Landwehr companies, the fortress sappers three Élite and sixteen Landwehr companies, and the pioneers six Élite and nine Landwehr companies.

Army service corps Army service corps duties were carried out by two distinct branches: transport work by the train, and commissariat work by the administrative (Verwaltungs) corps. The personnel of both branches were non-combatants.

Whether Switzerland could have survived involvement in a twentieth-century war is open to question, but there can be no doubt that her army would have fought to protect the country's neutrality and that in a defensive war it was fully capable of exploiting the marksmanship, endurance and mobility of its troops and the advantages of the national terrain.

V·THE VIEW FROM 1899

Towards the end of 1899 there was published in London a book called *The Armies of the World* by Charles S. Jerram which outlined the composition, strength and special characteristics of the armies of the powers, arranged alphabetically from Austria to the United States.

The account which Jerram gives of the relative strengths and positions of the armies of the late nineteenth century is taken from a viewpoint which is almost mid-way between the years 1854 and 1914, and as such records the process of change and development I have tried to describe. We are given an invaluable picture of contemporary world politics and the attitudes of governments to their armies. It is thus possible not only to compare details of specific organization and deployment then and now, but also to put into perspective the changes in international relations from a military point of view.

Jerram justified the book by the international reaction to the recent Russian peace proposals which, he said, 'the world had lately heard, with astonished cynicism or with languid interest'. These were the proposals which led to the Hague Conferences of 1899 and 1907, and some nebulous regulations for the civilized conduct of warfare. There was no limit to the level of the world's armaments.

Awaiting the outcome of the Conferences, Jerram addressed himself to the armies of the world, together with one or two ventures in prophecy. Of Austria, for example, he wrote:

The loosely-constructed fabric of the State is for the present kept together by bonds of mutual convenience and by respect for the ageing Emperor; but, in the ordinary course of things . . . one would expect that in time to come the German part of the State would join the German empire, and the remainder perhaps form a buffer state between an enlarged German empire and Russia. However this may be, the condition of things in the dual monarchy has for some while been critical, and some form of revolution is probably only a matter of time.

Looking ahead to future wars, the author doubted whether they will be more terrible than the wars of the past, or whether the armies of Europe are doing the countries to which they belong much mischief at present . . . In the matters of strategy, and even of tactics, there have been no changes in our own days more extraordinary than the changes, where any, in the past; and in the matter of expense, the expense of war does not appear to increase at a more dangerous rate than the expense of education, or than local expense, though all three, and many more, objects of expenditure are rightly eyed askance in the huge proportions which they have latterly assumed.

The detail into which Jerram went in dealing with the larger armies is shown by items from the chapter on Austria. Would-be officers, he stated, had to be approved by the officers of the regiment which they wished to join. In 1899 the total peace-time strength of the army was 350,000 officers and men, with 61,336 horses, while the strength on mobilization was 2,475,000 men, with 1792 guns. An extra 500,000 men could, it was estimated, be 'combed out' from various untrained groups. The active army on mobilization would consist of forty-four infantry and eight cavalry divisions. On mobilization 250,000 horses would be required.

Rations are carefully detailed: bread 30.8 oz, rice or preserved vegetables 4.9 oz, fresh beef 10.6 oz, salt 1 oz, tobacco 1.2 oz, 1/10 pint of brandy and 3/5 pint of wine. Horses had 6.17 lbs of hay and between 13 lbs and 14.8 lbs of oats, according to the kind of work which they were expected to do and whether they were riding horses, draught horses, etc.

The different uniforms of the various arms of the service are described, with attention to the details of military tailoring as practised seventy-five years ago.

The *infantry* single-breasted frock is of dark blue cloth . . . Dragoons and Uhlans wear a single-breasted tunic of light blue cloth (Hussars — light blue or dark blue). *Regiments* are shown by the colour of the collar cuffs and head-dress. The dolman, which is the same colour as the tunic, is lined with fur, and has a black astrakhan collar. The cloak is brown cloth with a large triangular hood. Pantaloons and high boots (Hussars — Hessian boots) are worn . . . Hungarian landwehr cavalry . . . the Csako (head-dress) has a straight white horse-hair plume.

On the march [Jerram continued] the usual pace is the quick march of 115 paces to the minute. The length of the pace (29.53 inches) is about the same as that of English infantry. At the double 160 paces per minute are taken.

Under the heading of Tactics a summary is given of the principal rules laid down by what must have been the Austrian equivalent of the British Field Service Regulations or the Infantry Training Manual.

Infantry — The real attack is usually on one flank, the frontal attack being merely to hold the enemy. The regiment is formed in firing line and reserves. The firing line is 1000 to 1100 paces beyond the regimental reserve . . . The advance in the firing line is usually in rushes of from 60 to 80 paces, advantage being taken of cover. Troops in the firing line can only advance and retire. Changes of front can only be effected by troops in reserve.

There is little infantry fire beyond 1000 paces or less; the infantry should as a rule be able to see distinctly the object aimed at . . . At 500 paces the attack proper is delivered, infantry and artillery pouring in an overwhelming fire, and reserves come up to the assault position, the whole force advances, magazine fire is opened, and, the final position having been reached, the whole body of the infantry charges with fixed bayonets. Until this position is reached the firing line does not fix bayonets.

In the present controversy in regard to the decisive firing it is worth noticing that Austria puts it at 500 paces, Russia at from 400 to 500 paces, Holland at over 700 paces etc.

Cavalry usually attack at right angles to a front, or obliquely against a flank . . . The order to attack is given at 1000 paces. The line advances at a trot, then breaks into a canter, and the charge is sounded at about eighty paces from the enemy.

Making his way through the armies of the powers Jerram next tackled that of Belgium. At the time when he wrote the Belgian army was perhaps the least considered in Europe: it was not intended that it should actually fight but only guard the frontiers and warn belligerents against violating Belgian neutrality by accident. Jerram foresaw that this attitude would not save Belgium from invasion:

. . . while by the Conventions of 1831 the *perpetual neutrality* of Belgium is guaranteed, these conventions state that such neutrality would be of little use to the neighbouring states if the kingdom fails in the military force to make it respected ... her wealth and sea-coast must be tempting; and besides, in case of war between Germany and France, it is considered probable that, with the enormous armies which would be brought into the field, use would be made of Belgian territory, since the available conterminous frontier of these states would not afford space enough for the efficient employment of the vast hosts concerned.

It was not until 1909 that King Leopold II, virtually on his deathbed, signed a law for the reorganization of the army, which introduced for the first time the principle of universal military service. Hitherto the army had been recruited on a voluntary basis, any shortage of volunteers being made up by the drawing of lots.

Those unlucky in the draw were able, up to the introduction of Leopold's reforms, to obtain substitutes on payment of £60. Out of 45,000 men, of twenty years of age, some 13,000 were enlisted annually.

A single page is devoted to the Brazilian army; 27,000 strong, it was partly recruited by voluntary enlistment and partly by ballot. The procedure of the ballot is explained in the 1911 edition of the *Encyclopaedia Britannica:* 'According to law military service is obligatory, but the government has been unable to enforce it. Impressment is commonly employed to fill the ranks and in cases of emergency the prison population is drawn upon for recruits.'

The Chinese army, which is also covered in one page, found Jerram in prophetic mood.

The Chinese Empire is about to share the fate of Africa. The present writer does not hold any illusions in regard to the reasons for such a fate. He does not believe that any country takes possession of parts of Africa or Asia in order to do the people in those places good, though good may occasionally result incidentally. England and Russia advance in Asia because having once started they cannot stop.

To attempt any estimate of the forces of China is impracticable. The *Black Flags,* formed on the nucleus of Gordon's Taiping army and trained by European officers, may, at their best, have numbered 50,000 men. But English officers of distinction believe that the Chinese soldier when trained will make an efficient fighter, and perhaps the best hope for the continued existence of the Chinese Empire consists in the possibility of China allowing some part of her forces to be trained by Anglo-Indian officers, seeing that England at present does not covet territory, only commerce, in that part of the world.

Of the Egyptian army Jerram writes: 'Among the results of British endeavour few have been more successful than the reformation in sixteen years of Egypt and the Egyptian army, by such men as Lord Cromer, Sir Evelyn Wood, Sir F. Grenfell and Lord Kitchener.'

Jerram completed his notes on the English army only a few weeks before the outbreak of the Second Boer War. This was to be the greatest test through which the army passed in the years between the Crimea and Ypres, and he was rather more optimistic than events were to justify: '... the British is the only army which has much serious practice in war ...' With the British colonial wars in mind he says:

The fact that the English officer, at least, has during the course of his career many more opportunities of war service than is the case with his continental brother, should render him a more efficient officer, and the same should be true, though to a less extent, of the British private, who frequently has opportunities of war service during his career in the active army.

The possibility of cuts being made in the £42 million spent annually on the land forces of the Empire, including India, is touched upon briefly:

There are, too, persons impertinent enough to desire more light to be thrown upon the expenditure on the War Office itself, and besides, upon the whole expenditure on civilians connected with the service ... An astonishing instance of what can be done ... is that we learn that one result of Mr Cardwell's reforms was the reduction of official correspondence from 1500 to 900 letters daily.

Supply has usually been a weak point in our Army system and seems to be so still.

Summing up his introduction, the author writes: 'We may look forward with confidence to the future, as we look back with pride upon the past of the armies of the Queen.' He sets the total war strength of these armies at 1,170,000.

New regulations introduced just prior to the writing of this book gave the British private the famous 'Queen's shilling' free of deductions for the first time. The daily ration apparently consisted of ¾ lb beef or mutton, including bone, 1 lb bread, flour, groceries, vegetables, etc. Lord Wolseley, noted Jerram, advocated making the field ration as palatable as possible: 'Cheese, jam and pickles should never be absent from the soldier's ration when it is possible to obtain these articles of food.' He also advocated the issue during campaigns of soap and tobacco rations, 1 lb of each per month.

With one of his looks ahead Jerram was right on target. 'Mounted infantry in the modern sense originated in the Secession War [American Civil War] and is one of the causes of the ultimate success of the North. A force is required ... which shall comprise mobility with the characteristics of infantry, especially in shooting.' Such a force eventually brought the Boer War to a successful conclusion; in Europe, however, it was believed that much of the work would be done by cyclists whose evolutions during the Easter manoeuvres of 1899 in Britain were 'highly commended by military authorities'.

Now, more than three-quarters of a century after Jerram wrote, we may forget that one of the vital problems for all armies in those days was the provision of sufficient horses. In the late nineteenth century, there were about three million horses in Britain and Ireland, of which 70,000 were fit for military purposes, and 60,000 at least, Jerram estimated, would be needed in war-time. As for the shortage of remounts and horses for transport, an earlier general remarked 'we will commence a great war with little means'. At this time it was planned that the field army, on mobilization, should consist of three army corps and four cavalry brigades with, behind them, perhaps thirty-three volunteer infantry brigades and eighty-four volunteer batteries.

'For the Foreign Expeditionary Force', said Jerram, '20,000 men are detailed and liberally equipped. The bulk of the force is at Aldershot, and equipment is divided between Aldershot and Southampton.'

According to Jerram all was far from well with France and her army.

With a monstrous load of debt, an almost stationary population, an overwhelming military despotism, and adventurous politicians who vie with one another in corruption and imbecility, France stands trembling on the brink of bankruptcy and a military revolution . . . Sacrificed towards the end of the eighteenth century by birth and money, France at the close of the nineteenth sorely needs a leisured plutocratic aristocracy to restore the balance of things.

According to Jerram, about 230,000 recruits were available each year for the standing army. Of these 69,000 served for one year and 161,000 for two to three years. In addition, about 16,000 volunteers joined the home army and 5000 the army in the colonies annually, giving a total strength of about 550,000 in peace-time. The total strength on mobilization for war was estimated by Jerram at 4,660,000; he adds, however, that this might not be the only force available during a long war. 'It is possible that . . . several million more untrained men would be called upon . . .' to replace casualties.

The housekeeping of the French army included several distinctive features. Ration scales provided for such items as nearly half a pint of wine, or a pint of beer or cider or half a gill of brandy which might be in addition to the wine, beer or cider. Tobacco ration was ½ oz per day of shag for NCOs and men and ¾ oz for officers. Of fuel to make coffee, each man was allowed 1⅔ oz wood and 1 oz of coal or charcoal. Each man carried a first-aid packet containing bandages, a field dressing, oiled silk and two safety pins. When rations were short, which was very seldom the case except under war conditions, recourse was had to requisitioning, which could only be carried out by force after beat of drum and the order given to all good citizens to withdraw.

After 1870, to facilitate French deployment the total length of railway lines was increased from 15,786 miles to 22,299 miles, and on mobilization 9959 locomotives and 293,465 carriages and wagons were available in 1899. According to Jerram, it was calculated that by the evening of the fifth day of mobilization the railways would be in a position to convey 5,796,000 men; 'a number' he comments 'very much larger than the total forces of France'.

The seeds of the enormous French losses of 1914 are found in a single sentence of Jerram's book; 'Drills, manoeuvres and military instruction generally are founded on the principle that the offensive alone permits of decisive results.' This basic principle of French military thought stemmed chiefly from the difference in size between the populations of France and Germany. At the end of the last century the population of France was 38,518,000 and of Germany 52,279,000. It was believed that this difference could only be compensated for by an all-out immediate offensive. This was also judged to be more suitable to the French temperament than a defensive battle.

Summing up the French army, Jerram concluded his survey with a quotation from Captain Danrit, writing in *L'Armée Française* in 1899: 'The enemy, the centuries-old enemy, from Joan of Arc down to the present day, and forever, is the Englishman.'

Jerram noted that the discipline and spirit of the German army were 'reported to be quite excellent'. Duelling was becoming less frequent, discouraged by the Emperor for slight causes and by the Church for all causes, 'yet there is no doubt that in Germany even the religiously-disposed young lady looks upon the thing as a necessity. Honour is first, religion second. Death for honour's sake may at times be necessary.'

Jerram was writing when the reaction against anti-German feeling in Britain, caused by the Kaiser's telegram of support to Kruger, was in full swing. 'Six months ago we were all anti-German; however, today we are all pro-German. The Kaiser speaks of "our common race". Mr Rhodes visits Berlin. The *rapprochement* seems sagacious. The two nations have much to do all over the world that had best be done together.'

The peace strength of the German army when Jerram wrote was 545,000 and its war strength 3,013,000. In addition there was a so-called reserve army of 3,200,000, only about half a million of whom had received military training for, at this time, a total of less than one-third of available manpower was being called up. Altogether the total of the enrolled German forces, trained and untrained, was 6,213,000 which, incidentally, is rather less than half the total the Germans mobilized during the years 1914-18.

Following their victories against Denmark, Austria and France, the Germans had very definite ideas as to how wars were to be waged in the future. According to Jerram, in battle it was laid down

The artillery clears the way, and the infantry gets as close as possible to the enemy's position before opening fire. So soon as the enemy's fire begins to weaken, the ranks close up, magazine fire commences, and with bugles sounding and drums beating, the troops march quickly upon the enemy, cheering as they go.

The essence of success is rapidity combined with order and with security from counter-attack. Hence cavalry will seldom attack infantry which has not been previously shaken. The charge is delivered in one unbroken line of two closed-up ranks. At the shock the trumpets sound and the men shout Hurrah! In pursuit the object is always to remain engaged, and keep the enemy from rallying. A sure test of discipline is rapidity in assembling after the *mêlée* in informal detachments of two ranks . . . In action against other cavalry the essential thing is to obtain the initiative, and compel the enemy to defence . . . Artillery is attacked if possible, in front or rear.

When *The Armies of the World* was written the Italian army was just beginning to recover from its defeat in Abyssinia. This had been the result, in part, of the vastly over-ambitious way in which the new kingdom of Italy had tried to equip itself with the armaments and colonial territories of a first-class power. Not only had too much been spent, but, hints Jerram, it had not always been used wisely or honestly, so that figures on Italy's armed forces do 'not always represent very strong facts'. All Italian men, in theory, were liable to military service, but about 67% of them passed straight into the reserve without any military training at all. The total peace strength of the army at this time was 222,000. The strength, including trained reserves, which could be reached in war was theoretically 738,200, with 2,500,000 untrained men liable for service.

An interesting point in Jerram's book is that it is not until this point that he has thought it worth mentioning the existence of machine guns. He now records the fact that the Italians have double-barrelled machine guns as part of the armament of some fortresses.

On Japan, Jerram was very brief, writing between the Sino-Japanese War of 1894-5 and the Russo-Japanese War ten years later, both resounding successes for the Japanese. He says: 'Japan — the England of the East, as it has sometimes been called — seems destined to play a considerable, though not a decisive, part in the re-arrangement of Eastern Asia. For *her* the best chance is an alliance with England, for us such an alliance would be of doubtful omen.' At the end of the Chinese War, the Japanese army numbered 70,000 men, organized in six divisions, with 200,000 reserves. Jerram remarks that it was intended, at the time of his writing, to maintain a peace strength of twelve divisions, totalling 145,000 men, with a war strength of 520,000, and he comments:

The training of officers at the military college and academy is highly commended by competent European authorities. The army system is to a considerable extent that of Germany, and some of the Japanese officers have been trained in Germany and other European countries. Rifles and guns are, many of them, manufactured at home on the best European models. The war indemnity of £38,000,000 exacted from China has been expended on naval and military preparations, but it has not proved sufficient, and Japan is indulging in increased debt.

The army for which Jerram had the greatest admiration, and perhaps affection, is clearly that of Montenegro, a mountainous kingdom which was incorporated in Yugoslavia in 1918. In 1899:

This plucky little state has a population of about 250,000 ... The army organization is tribal. The service is for thirty years, but everybody fights as much and as long as he can. The *war strength* may be 43,000 men.
Uniform — The only regulation article is a small, round, black, brimless cap with a red top [on which was worn the badge of rank].
Armament — in 1895 the Tsar presented Montenegro with 30,000 Berdan rifles, 15,000,000 cartridges and six Gatling guns ...
Mobilization, by word of mouth, telegraph and bugle call, is very rapid. In 1887, 6000 men were mobilized on the Austrian frontier between 8 p.m. and 4 a.m. Every man answers to the call as their ancestors have done for some hundreds of past years. Long may it be so.

Jerram turns from one of the smallest armies of Europe to the biggest: 'Of all foreign armies, the Russian is the most interesting to the English people,' he says. Service with the colours lasted four to five years and above 1,200,000 men were liable to be called up.

However the actual annual intake was about 400,000 so that the total peace establishment apparently was 36,000 officers and 860,000 men, but neither British nor German authorities were able to name a definite figure. The war strength was thought to be about four million on mobilization with a much larger number available as the war continued.

In Europe and the Caucasus the active army was planned to take the field with twenty-four army corps, comprising fifty-one infantry and twenty-three cavalry divisions as well as two rifle brigades. In 1899, on the eve of the Russo-Japanese War, there were no units larger than brigades in Asia.

Regulations laid down that infantry attacks would be made with closed ranks, cheering at fifty paces distance. No provision was made for an advance faster than quick march. This was a tactical error, Jerram pointed out, in the opinion of some authorities who complained that losses must be heavy under an advance on open ground, such as the Russian plains.

The Russian army was equipped with a certain number of automatic weapons, ten-barrelled Gatling machine guns and one-barrelled Maxim 'automatic machine guns', but it does not seem to have been revealed how many of each there were, nor is the composition given of 'an international balloon park', also mentioned.

Jerram envisaged three different areas of conflict between Russia and Britain: the first in northern Scandinavia, with British action, which he regards as improbable, in defence of the Norwegian warm water ports; second, another British attack on Sevastopol; and third, collision between the expanding British and Russian spheres of influence in Asia.

The book then continues with the armies of the South African republics, that is the Transvaal and the Orange Free State, the combined strength of which is estimated at 46,500. In fact, when the Second Boer War came, a few weeks after the book was finished, it would seem that the total forces of the two republics actually amounted to 35,000. Of these the only units existing in peace-time were the artillery of the two republics — which consisted of about forty modern guns and four machine guns.

When Jerram made his survey of the United States army the Spanish-American War was just over. Hostilities, however, continued in the Philippines between the Americans and the Filipinos fighting for immediate independence. 'In the modern sense the army of the United States can scarcely yet be said to exist.' Shortcomings had been revealed by the war and the failure of supply and medical services is indicated by the published figures of casualties:

Killed in action	329
Died of wounds	125
Died of disease	5,277

Voluntary service in the regular army at this time was for five years. The peace strength of the army in 1899 was limited to 2147 officers and 25,710 men, organized as follows:

Commanders of the international forces in Peking in 1910. Left to right: Russian, British, Russian, French, British, Japanese, German, French, Austrian, Italian, American and British.

Infantry	25 regiments, of 8 companies each
Cavalry	10 regiments, of 10 troops or half squadrons each
Artillery	5 regiments, of 12 batteries each

Engineer and Signal units

In the same year it was proposed to increase the regular army to 100,000 of which 30,000 were intended for operations in the Philippines.

In many ways, 1899 was the ideal time for such a survey, but perhaps the most interesting part of Jerram's book transcends the period of which he writes, and it is his view of war that provides an admirable conclusion.

As has often been pointed out, the strategy of war has always been the same. The General desires to get as quickly as possible into the best position for striking the first, and that an effective blow, and in all ages he has attained this end by following much the same rules. There are certain convenient methods of concentration existing in the present, such as railways, which did not exist in the past, and there are means too of ascertaining information quickly, and of giving information quickly, such as the telegraph, which enable the Commander-in-Chief to be further away from the seat of war, than could have been the case in the days of Caesar; but could Caesar return to lead the armies of France or Germany, his aims and objects would still be those of the Gallic War. He would still get his armies into position for the fight by following the rules of the game in the past.

INDEX

INDEX